MOUNT VERNON

A HANDBOOK

THE MOUNT VERNON LADIES' ASSOCIATION
OF THE UNION, MOUNT VERNON, VIRGINIA

GEORGE WASHINGTON'S BOOKPLATE,
ENGRAVED FOR HIM IN LONDON IN 1772,
INCORPORATED THE WASHINGTON FAMILY COAT-OF-ARMS.

THE WASHINGTON FAMILY

BY EDWARD SAVAGE—1796

The artist has portrayed General and Mrs. Washington with their two wards, George Washington Parke Custis and Eleanor Parke Custis, grand-children of Martha Washington by her first marriage. In the background a servant in the red-and-buff Washington livery waits in attendance. The map, to which Mrs. Washington points with her fan, is of the "Capital City," then being developed on the banks of the Potomac. Savage made copper plate engravings of this painting in 1798, four of which were pur-chased by General Washington. One of these originals may be seen in the small dining room. THE NATIONAL GALLERY OF ART, ANDREW W. MELLON COLLECTION

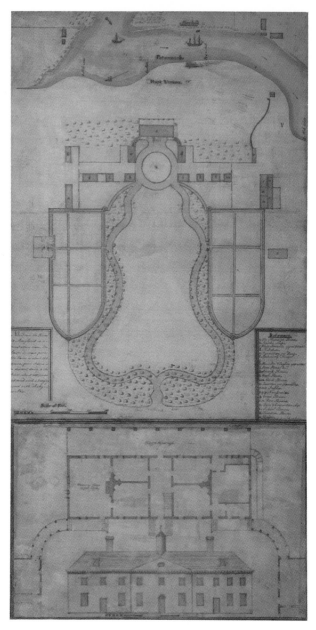

THE VAUGHAN PLAN OF MOUNT VERNON, PRESENTED TO GEN-
ERAL WASHINGTON BY SAMUEL VAUGHAN IN NOVEMBER 1787.
THE PLAN IS BASED ON NOTES MADE BY VAUGHAN IN JUNE OF THAT
YEAR, AND ITS ACCURACY IS ATTESTED BY GENERAL WASHING-
TON'S LETTER OF ACKNOWLEDGMENT.

CONTENTS

A BRIEF WASHINGTON-MOUNT VERNON CHRONOLOGY___8

A BRIEF HISTORICAL PREFACE___11

THE MOUNT VERNON FARMS___16

THE GARDENS AND GROUNDS___22

THE MANSION___32

THE LARGE DINING ROOM___40

THE PASSAGE___50

THE LITTLE PARLOR___54

THE WEST PARLOR___57

THE SMALL DINING ROOM___62

THE DOWNSTAIRS BEDROOM___66

THE UPPER CHAMBERS___68

GENERAL AND MRS. WASHINGTON'S BEDCHAMBER___76

THE STUDY___80

THE PANTRY___88

THE COURTYARD OUTBUILDINGS___90

THE KITCHEN___92

THE MUSEUM___98

PLANTATION LIFE___106

THE STABLE___114

THE TOMB___118

GEORGE WASHINGTON: PIONEER FARMER___121

THE MOUNT VERNON LADIES' ASSOCIATION OF THE UNION___125

A BRIEF WASHINGTON-CUSTIS GENEALOGY___129

A CONJECTURAL EVOLUTION OF THE MANSION___130

MEASURED DRAWINGS OF THE MANSION___131

A PERSPECTIVE VIEW OF MOUNT VERNON___132

A BRIEF WASHINGTON– MOUNT VERNON CHRONOLOGY

1674	John Washington, great-grandfather of George, is granted the Mount Vernon homesite.
1726	Augustine Washington, father of George, acquires the Mount Vernon property from his sister, Mildred.
1732	George, first child of Augustine and Mary (Ball) Washington, born at the family place on the Potomac River in Westmoreland County, Virginia.
1735–39	Augustine Washington in residence at Mount Vernon with his young family.
1743	Augustine Washington dies. Lawrence Washington, George's elder half brother, marries and settles at Mount Vernon.
1752	Lawrence Washington dies at Mount Vernon.
1754	George Washington acquires Mount Vernon by lease from Lawrence Washington's widow.
1759	George Washington marries Martha Dandridge Custis, widow of Daniel Parke Custis, and settles at Mount Vernon with his wife and two young stepchildren, John Parke and Martha Parke Custis.

CHARLES WILLSON PEALE, 1776

Martha Washington

1761	Inherits Mount Vernon following the death of Lawrence Washington's widow.
1775	Elected General to command all Continental forces.
1781	Stops briefly at Mount Vernon en route to and from Yorktown. John Parke Custis dies; the Washingtons take in his two youngest children, Eleanor Parke and George Washington Parke Custis.
1783	Resigns his commission to Congress and retires to Mount Vernon.
1787	Presides over the Constitutional Convention in Philadelphia.
1789–97	Years of the presidency. Visits Mount Vernon fifteen times.
1799	Dies and is entombed in the old family vault.
1802	Martha Washington dies and is entombed beside her husband. Mount Vernon passes to Washington's nephew Bushrod Washington.
1829	Bushrod Washington dies, leaving Mount Vernon to his nephew John Augustine Washington.
1853	Mount Vernon Ladies' Association founded by Ann Pamela Cunningham of South Carolina to purchase and preserve the home and tomb of George Washington.
1858	Mount Vernon Ladies' Association receives its final charter from the Commonwealth of Virginia and purchases Mount Vernon from John A. Washington, Jr.

A Brief Historical Preface

No estate in United America is more pleasantly situated than this. It lies in a high, dry and healthy Country 300 miles by water from the Sea, . . . on one of the finest Rivers in the world. . . . It is situated in a latitude between the extremes of heat and cold, and is the same distance by land and water, with good roads and the best navigation [to and] from the Federal City, Alexandria and George town; distant from the first twelve, from the second nine, and from the last sixteen miles.

Time and circumstance have wrought no changes to qualify or invalidate the foregoing description of Mount Vernon from a letter written by George Washington to an English correspondent in 1793. Mount Vernon stands as a monument to its builder, *pleasantly situated* on a commanding eminence, overlooking the Potomac and the low Maryland hills. The tree-crowned hilltop, the wide sweep of the river, and the wooded shores beyond present a prospect of unchanged beauty.

The rivers of Virginia were broad avenues offering easy access to a rich interior, and their shores were rapidly settled after the first precarious years in the history of the colony. George Washington's great-grandfather, John Washington, was a pioneer settler of the Northern Neck (the area between the Potomac and the Rappahannock rivers). This ancestor, the emigrant, established himself along the lower Potomac in Westmoreland County about 1657. In 1674, John Washington and Nicholas Spencer were granted five thousand acres of land along the upper Potomac, between Dogue and Little Hunting creeks, by Thomas, Lord Culpeper, proprietor of the Northern Neck under dispensation of his patron, King Charles II. The grantees were obliged to pay an annual quit rent in perpetuity and "to seat and plant" the land within three years. In 1690, the tract was divided between Lawrence, son of John Washington, and the heirs of Nicholas

11

Phil.^a, June 23^d., 1775

My dearest,
    As I am within a few Minutes of leaving this City, I could
not think of departing from it without dropping you a line, especially
as I do not know whether it may be in my power to write again till
I get to the Camp at Boston—I go fully trusting in that Providence
which has been more bountiful to me than I deserve, & in full
confidence of a happy meeting with you sometime in the Fall—I
have not time to add more, as I am surrounded with Company to
take leave of me—I retain an unalterable affection for you, which
neither time or distance can change my best love to Jack & Nelly,
& regards for the rest of the Family concludes me with the utmost
truth & sincerity

Y^r. entire G^o: Washington

Spencer. From Lawrence, the Washington half of the grant, then known as Hunting Creek Plantation, passed to a daughter, Mildred. In 1726 Augustine Washington, father of George, purchased the Little Hunting Creek Plantation from his sister, Mildred, and her husband, Roger Gregory. In 1735, when George Washington was three years old, Augustine removed his family from their plantation on Pope's Creek (now officially designated Washington's birthplace) in Westmoreland County to the Hunting Creek Plantation. Four years later he moved once again, establishing his household at the Ferry Farm, on the Rappahannock River near Fredericksburg.

In 1740 Augustine Washington deeded the Little Hunting Creek Plantation to his son Lawrence, who had just come of age. By the time of his marriage in 1743, Lawrence had settled on the estate and had renamed it in honor of Admiral Edward Vernon, under whom he had served in the Caribbean. Augustine Washington died in 1743, and his young son George spent a part of his youth with his elder half brother at Mount Vernon. In 1752, Lawrence died, and two years later George Washington came into possession of Mount Vernon by purchase of the life interest of his brother's widow. When she died in 1761, Washington inherited the estate.

The history of this early period is poorly recorded. It must be drawn or deduced principally from wills, title papers, and archaeological evidence. It was not known until the first vestry book of Truro Parish was discovered, about the turn of this century, that George Washington's father had resided at Mount Vernon. In the absence of this information, it had been assumed that the central portion of the present house was built by Lawrence Washington in 1743. The vestry book revealed that Augustine Washington was a vestryman of Truro Parish, in which Mount Vernon is situated, in 1735 and for several years thereafter. Supplementary evidence, since brought to light, establishes the fact that he resided at Mount Vernon from 1735 until 1739. It is also recorded that Lawrence Washington's inheritance included a "patrimonial Mansion." The survival of this early structure within the fabric of the present house is confirmed by a diarist, who in 1801 identified the central portion of the house as having been "constructed by the General's father."

From 1752 until 1759, George Washington's military service, as aide to General Braddock and as commander of Virginia militia, permitted only infrequent visits to Mount Vernon. During this period the plantation was managed by his younger brother, John Augustine. Fort Duquesne fell in November 1758, and George Washington retired to private life. In January

---

FACING PAGE: SHORTLY BEFORE HER DEATH, MARTHA WASHINGTON DESTROYED HER CORRESPONDENCE WITH HER HUSBAND; ONLY TWO LETTERS OF GEORGE TO MARTHA, EITHER OVERLOOKED OR DELIBERATELY SPARED, ARE KNOWN TO SURVIVE. BOTH DATE FROM THE PERIOD IMMEDIATELY FOLLOWING WASHINGTON'S APPOINTMENT AS COMMANDER-IN-CHIEF OF THE CONTINENTAL ARMY IN JUNE OF 1775. THE LETTER SHOWN HERE, ONE OF THE GREAT TREASURES OF THE MOUNT VERNON MANUSCRIPT COLLECTION, WAS WRITTEN JUST MOMENTS BEFORE GENERAL WASHINGTON SET OUT ON A JOURNEY THAT WOULD LEAD THROUGH PERIL TO VICTORY AND A SHINING PLACE IN HISTORY.

1759, he married Martha Dandridge Custis, widow of Daniel Parke Custis. To an English friend he wrote, *I am now, I believe, fixed at this Seat with an agreeable Consort for Life and hope to find more happiness in retirement than I ever experienced amidst a wide and bustling World.* This expectation of retirement was to be disappointed, but the peaceful years together at Mount Vernon before the Revolutionary War were the happiest of their lives. There is an echo of this in the lines George Washington wrote to his wife from Philadelphia in 1775, on the eve of his departure for New England as newly appointed Commander-in-Chief of the Continental Army: *I should enjoy more real happiness in one month with you at home than I have the most distant prospect of finding abroad, if my stay were to be seven times seven years.*

During the war years Martha Washington spent eight winters with her husband in his northern encampments, from the first at Cambridge to the last at Newburgh, leaving Mount Vernon in the late autumn and returning in the spring as the opening guns announced a new military campaign. George Washington stopped briefly at Mount Vernon en route to and from Yorktown in 1781. Lund Washington, distant cousin and faithful friend, managed the estate in his absence. General Washington resigned his commission at Annapolis in December 1783, and returned to Mount Vernon. Once again he looked forward to the life of a private citizen and husbandman on the bank of the Potomac, but again he was disappointed. He remained at Mount Vernon until he assumed the presidency in 1789, but

his fame and inevitable position as leader in the movement for a stronger union denied him the domestic ease he desired.

In the eight years of his presidency, George Washington visited Mount Vernon fifteen times, remaining for periods that varied from several days to several months. On his retirement in March 1797, he returned home once again and, in the two and one-half years that remained to him, he enjoyed a greater degree of the tranquillity he had so long desired. He died on December 14, 1799. Mrs. Washington survived until May 1802.

In the forty-five years of George Washington's tenure Mount Vernon grew in size from 2,126 acres to approximately eight thousand. By the terms of his will, this estate was divided after the death of Mrs. Washington. The Mansion and four thousand acres were inherited by Washington's nephew Bushrod, while the rest of the estate passed to other heirs. From Bushrod Washington, Mount Vernon ultimately descended to John Augustine Washington, Jr., a great-grandnephew of General Washington, who conveyed the property to the Mount Vernon Ladies' Association in 1858.

On this rout you traverse a considerable wood, and after having passed over two hills, you discover a country house of an elegant and majestic simplicity.

J. P. Brissot de Warville, 1788

THE MOUNT VERNON FARMS

George Washington's Mount Vernon estate of eight thousand acres was divided into five farms, each a complete unit with its own overseers, work force of slaves, livestock, equipment, and buildings. The Mansion House Farm was not a farm in the usual sense of the word; no large-scale cultivation of field crops was carried on around the *home house*. The master's plans for this area are indicated in a sentence from a letter to his manager: *I do not hesitate to confess, that reclaiming, and laying the grounds down handsomely to grass, and in woods thinned or in clumps, about the Mansion House is among my first objects and wishes.* This area of about five hundred acres around the Mansion was developed as a gentleman's country seat, a new world version of an English country house of the period. Within a deep border of woods were rolling meadows, vistas, and groves of trees. Between the Mansion and the river shore was an extensive park; below the kitchen garden was an enclosed vineyard. Small areas were cultivated, but these were usually restricted to testing new crops and agricultural methods. The roughly five hundred acres owned by the Mount Vernon Ladies' Association corresponds closely to the borders of the Mansion House Farm. Much of what was open land in Washington's time is today heavily wooded. The four outlying farms no longer exist. They were divided by the terms of Washington's will and have since been many times subdivided. Nothing remains to mark them save scattered bricks, where buildings once

16

stood, and the ditch banks, which defined field boundaries. Yet in Washington's time these four farms, River, Muddy Hole, Dogue, and Union, were the focus of intensive agricultural activity. As many as two hundred slaves and other workers lived on the farms and more than three thousand acres were actually under cultivation. There were brick barns on some of the farms, which were not excelled by any of that period in America; one, a sixteen-sided structure designed by George Washington, had a unique threshing floor in the loft.

To a friend General Washington wrote:

my agricultural pursuits and rural amusements . . . has been the most pleasing occupation of my life, and the most congenial to my temper, notwithstanding that a small proportion of it has been spent in this way.

Despite the burdens of the public career that diverted his attention from Mount Vernon, George Washington is acknowledged to have been one of the most progressive farmers in eighteenth-century America. Throughout his life, he was an agricultural pioneer, constantly experimenting with new crops and sophisticated techniques while working to improve farming in the entire country. When he took on the management of Mount Vernon in

From Monday 13th until Monday the 27th I remained at home; and spent my time in daily rides to my severl. farms and in receiving many visits.
Diary of George Washington, June 1791

A MAP OF THE FIVE MOUNT VERNON FARMS, SURVEYED AND DRAWN BY GEORGE WASHING-
TON IN 1793. THE MANSION HOUSE FARM APPEARS IN THE LOWER CENTER. GENERAL
WASHINGTON'S CALCULATIONS REVEAL THAT 3,260 ACRES OF THE 8,000-ACRE ESTATE
WERE ACTUALLY UNDER CULTIVATION. EACH OF THE FARMS HAD ITS OWN OVERSEER AND
WORK FORCE AS WELL AS BUILDINGS, LIVESTOCK, AND EQUIPMENT.

The more I am acquainted with agricultural affairs the more I am pleased with them. . . . I am led to reflect how much more delightful to an undebauched mind is the task of making improvements on the earth, than all to vain glory which can be acquired from ravaging it, by the most uninterrupted career of conquests.

George Washington to Arthur Young, December 4, 1788

THE WEST GATE OF MOUNT VERNON

the 1750s, George Washington decided to raise tobacco, the traditional staple crop that had dominated Virginia society and economy for more than a century. Tobacco cultivation was disadvantageous in several important respects, as Washington soon discovered. As a crop, it depleted the soil, and as a commodity, it depended on an uncertain and distant foreign market. Observing its ill effects, he began to seek new crops to replace tobacco. In the end, it was wheat that eclipsed tobacco as the principal Mount Vernon crop. And by 1767, he had abandoned the leaf altogether. The shift was one of profound importance for Mount Vernon and its master. Washington had become a farmer, producing grains and food crops, rather than a planter locked into a single staple. The shift to farming allowed him to introduce more innovative practices such as crop rotation and intensive plowing. He began to engage in the agricultural experimentation that would fascinate him for the rest of his life. By the time he was called away to take command of the Continental Army in 1775, Mount Vernon was a thriving agricultural enterprise. Washington's eight-year absence during the war interrupted its progress.

It was after the Revolutionary War that George Washington began his correspondence with several leading English agronomists. From them he imported not only ideas but also skilled workmen, new crops, and equipment. Not satisfied with the three-year crop rotation he had been using, he designed complex six- and ten-year systems. He also experimented tirelessly with fertilizers and crops. By the end of his life, he had raised, or at least tested, as many as sixty different crops. During periods of residence at Mount Vernon, Washington personally directed activities on the farms. It was his custom to make a daily tour of inspection, a horseback ride of some twenty miles. On Saturdays, his managers, including the

I begin my diurnal course with the Sun; if my hirelings are not in their places at that time I send them messages expressive of my sorrow for their indisposition; then having put these wheels in motion, I examine the state of things further; and the more they are probed, the deeper I find the wounds are which my buildings have sustained by an absence and neglect of eight years; by the time I have accomplished these matters, breakfast . . . is ready. This over, I mount my horse and ride around my farms, which employs me until it is time to dress for dinner.

George Washington to James McHenry, May 29, 1797

overseers of the four farms and the specialized work crews, such as carpenters, gardeners, and blacksmiths, would report to Washington on the week's activities. Some of these reports, transcribed by Washington or a secretary, have survived and form valuable resources for research. During the eight years of the presidency, reports were sent weekly by post to the seat of government with the manager's covering letter. The President responded at length each week, questioning omissions and discrepancies, cautioning, directing, and exhorting.

It is commonly assumed that George Washington was a wealthy man, and it would seem reasonable to expect that his farms would have produced a considerable income. The record belies that assumption. The farm ledger for the year 1798 credits the four outlying farms and related activities with a profit, but most of this was canceled out by the expense of maintaining the Mansion House Farm. The favorable balance for the year was less than twenty-seven hundred dollars. Similar figures are not available for other periods, but it is apparent from the record that 1798 was not a bad year. Poor soil, indifferent labor, and dilatory overseers were limiting factors every year. The prevailing system required an owner's close supervision if he were to prosper. After 1775, George Washington was not able to devote his full time to his own affairs, and they suffered from his lengthy absences from Mount Vernon. His income was never large, even before the Revolutionary War. His responsibilities were extensive and his impulses generous. In view of the circumstances, it would be accurate to say that George Washington sacrificed potential wealth to serve his country.

I think with you that the life of a Husbandman of all others is the most delectable. It is honorable. It is amusing, and, with judicious management, it is profitable.
George Washington to Alexander Spotswood, February 13, 1788

21

The Gardens and Grounds

The landscaped area of gardens and lawns around the Mansion is separated from the surrounding fields on three sides by sunken walls or *ha-has*. The outer walls of the formal gardens and the park wall on the river side complete the enclosure. The bowling green entrance and flanking ha-ha walls mark the boundary on the west between the formal and the informal areas.

The bowling green was a feature of the plan conceived and begun by General Washington shortly before the Revolutionary War. Some phases of the plan were carried forward during the war years, but development of the bowling green was not begun until early in 1785. The master of Mount Vernon himself supervised the work. His diary contains frequent references to the grading of the central lawn area and the transplanting of young trees and shrubs from the adjacent woods to the "Shrubberies" and "Wildernesses," which border the broad expanse of lawn on each side. His planting plan for the trees bordering the driveways was published in 1859; the original has since disappeared. Several of the larger trees now growing

Road to my Mill Swamp . . . and to other places in search of the sort of Trees I shall want for my Walks, groves and Wildernesses.
Diary of George Washington, January 12, 1785

22

ABOVE: VIEW FROM THE GREENHOUSE TOWARD THE MANSION. *FACING PAGE:* THE UPPER GARDEN.

THE UPPER GARDEN

on the bowling green can be identified as having been planted by Washington at this time.

George Washington's appreciation of trees is frequently revealed in his writings. From New York in August 1776, he wrote to his manager of his plan for:

groves of Trees at each end of the dwelling House, . . . these Trees to be Planted without any order or regularity (but pretty thick, as they can at any time be thin'd) and to consist that at the North end, of locusts altogether, and that at the South, of all the clever kinds of Trees (especially flowering ones) that can be got.

The grove at the north end of the Mansion was a prominent feature for many years and is now represented by a thriving restoration replanting (1934) of locusts, whose blossoms each spring justify George Washington's preference for the tree.

The sweeping panorama of the Potomac and the Maryland shore opposite Mount Vernon was itself an element of Washington's landscape design. The trees in the deer park on the slope leading from the Mansion to the river were maintained as a low "hanging grove" to set off the view. The vistas to the north and south of the Mansion were also kept open.

The formal gardens, the vineyard, and other planted areas around the Mansion were under the direction and care of a gardener, usually a

I have no objection to any sober or orderly person's gratifying their curiosity in viewing the buildings, Gardens &ct about Mount Vernon.
George Washington to William Pearce, November 23, 1794

FACING PAGE: LOCUST TREES IN THE NORTH GROVE.

Scotsman or a German, who had "signed articles" to serve in that capacity for three or more years in return for his passage, a stipulated annual wage and benefits.

The upper garden (flower garden) and lower garden (kitchen garden) are symmetrically placed on each side of the bowling green. The upper garden is dominated by its boxwood hedges. The only documentary clue to the origin and age of these hedges is contained in the gardener's weekly reports for 1798. He reports "digging and planting box edging." This box edging, by continuous growth through the intervening years, has become the principal feature of the garden, forming both edging and background for the beds. The domestic records identify the ornamental trees and shrubs, the fruits, and the vegetables that were planted in the gardens and about the grounds, but flowers are nowhere listed; in the absence of this specific information, the present planting list is restricted to annuals and perennials known to have been grown in Virginia gardens of the period. Fruits were cultivated in both the upper and lower gardens.

In 1785, General Washington built a handsome greenhouse, fronting the upper garden on the north side. A visitor described it as:

a complete Green-house which at this season is a vast, a great source of pleasure. Plants from every part of the world seem to flourish in the neatly

BELOW: THE GREENHOUSE AND QUARTERS IN THE UPPER GARDEN. *FACING PAGE:* THE UPPER GARDEN.

Plan of LOWER GARDEN

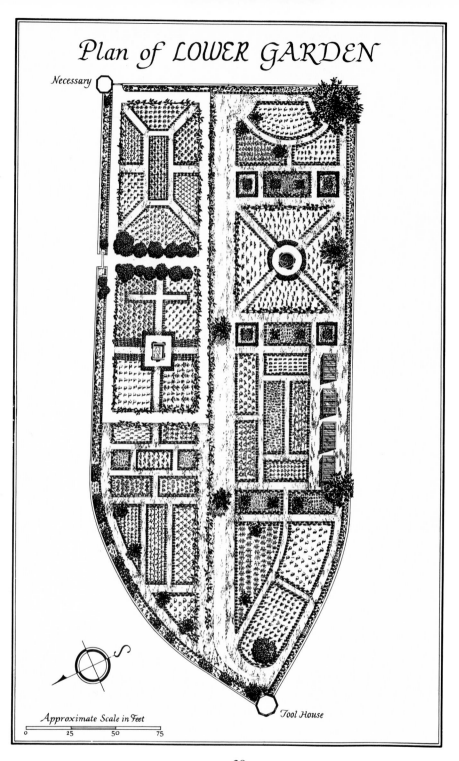

Necessary

Tool House

Approximate Scale in Feet

0   25   50   75

28

finished apartment, & from the arrangement of the whole, I conclude that it is managed by a skilful hand but whose I cannot tell—neither the General nor Mrs. W—seem more interested in it than the visitors.

The greenhouse and the flanking slave quarters were destroyed by fire in 1835. The present structures on the same site are reconstructions based on studied correlation of documentary and physical evidence.

The plan of the restored lower garden was derived from the same books on gardening that were owned and studied by George Washington. The vegetables, fruits, and herbs now grown in the garden are noted in his own writings and in the weekly reports of the gardener. Precedent for the fruit trees, which are trained against the garden walls (espaliers) and along the walks (cordons), is found in these records. The dipping cisterns conform with the ancient custom of exposing water to sunlight and air "that it may be soften'd thereby; for such Water as is taken out of Wells, Etc. just as it is used, is by no Means proper for any Sort of Plants." The following description of the formal planted area about the Mansion is taken from the diary of Julian Niemcewicz, a compatriot of Kosciusko, who spent twelve days at Mount Vernon in June 1798:

Tell the Gardener I shall expect everything that a Garden ought to produce, in the most ample manner.

George Washington to William Pearce, June 5, 1796

In the evening G[eneral] Washington showed us round his garden. It is well cultivated, perfectly kept, and is quite in English style. All the vegetables indispensable for the kitchen were found there.

Different kinds of berries—currants, raspberries, strawberries, gooseberries—a great quantity of peaches and cherries, but much inferior to ours; they are destroyed by robins, blackbirds, . . . before they are ripe. There were very many beautiful trees: the tulip-tree with flowers like the tulips, white with an orange touch at the base; magnolias with flowers whose scent is almost as strong as the smell of an orange-tree, but not so pleasant; the sweeter scent—the small violet flowers have the pleasantest smell I have ever noticed, a mixture of strawberries and pineapple; the splendid catalpa is not yet in flower; the New Scotland spruce of beautiful dark green, and many other trees and shrubs, covered with flowers of different hues, planted so as to produce the best of color-effects. The weeping-willows were deprived of their best decoration: the amount of snow was so great last winter that their boughs were broken under its weight.

The whole plantation, the garden, and the rest prove well that a man born with natural taste may guess a beauty without having ever seen its model. The General has never left America; but when one sees his house and his home and his garden it seems as if he had copied the best samples of the grand old homesteads of England.

THE LOWER GARDEN

Towards the East of the Mansion Nature has lavished magnificence, nor has Art interfered but to exhibit her to advantage. . . . Down the steep slope trees and shrubs are thickly planted. They are kept so low as not to interrupt the view but merely to furnish an agreeable border to the extensive prospect beyond. The mighty Potowmac runs close under this bank the elevation of which must be perhaps 250 feet.

Benjamin Henry Latrobe, July 19, 1796

30

FACING PAGE: NECESSARY IN THE LOWER GARDEN

THE MANSION

The will of George Washington's grandfather, Lawrence Washington, probated in 1698, reveals that tenants were then living at the Little Hunting Creek Plantation, later to be known as Mount Vernon. Their place of habitation is not known, but there is evidence of an earlier house in the basement walls of the present structure. The Mount Vernon cornerstone, removed from a cellar wall for better preservation and now displayed in the museum, bears the initials L. W. and a curious design, suggestive of the seventeenth century, but it is undated and cannot be definitely assigned to Lawrence, the grandfather of George. George also had a half brother named Lawrence, who preceded him as proprietor of Mount Vernon. In the absence of more definite evidence, this first chapter in the history of Mount Vernon cannot be completely reported, although the available facts suggest

that a tenant house, or quarter, was built on the site of the present Mansion by George Washington's grandfather.

The dwelling acquired by George Washington after the death of his elder half brother was of modest size and typical of its locality and period. It was one and one-half stories high with a central hall and four small rooms on the first floor. (Drawings of the conjectured evolution of the Mansion are to be found on page 125.) This nucleus of the present structure had been built by Augustine Washington, who resided here on his Hunting Creek Plantation for several years in the 1730s with his second wife, Mary Ball, and their young family, the eldest of whom was George.

In 1759, Mount Vernon acquired a mistress, and the master's correspondence for the preceding period of several years records the enlargement of his modest villa in anticipation of the event. The house was raised from one and one-half to two and one-half stories and was extensively redecorated. While the work was in progress, George Washington was absent on military duty, and the builder was supervised by a neighbor,

33

William Fairfax of Belvoir, an adjoining estate. Correspondence with Fairfax and others records the progress of improvements. Invoices of the period list the hardware and tools necessary to such a project, all of which had to be imported from the mother country. This pre–Revolutionary War house had its dependencies, gardens, and planted areas. The outbuildings were fewer in number and smaller; the gardens were less extensive than they now are. No ground plan or comprehensive description of the country seat at this stage in its development has survived. An entry in the master's diary reveals that the house had four principal dependencies, and that they were connected to the main house by "Pallisades" on low brick walls.

In 1773, George Washington made plans for additions to each end of the "Great house" and ordered materials from England. In July of the following summer he wrote to a friend, *I am very much engaged in raising one of the additions to my house, which I think (perhaps it is fancy) goes on better whilst I am present, than in my absence from the workmen.* These additions were part of a larger plan, which contemplated replacement of existing outbuildings with larger structures, creation of service lanes, development of the bowling green, and enlargement of the formal gardens. In May 1775, before the interior of the first Mansion addition was finished, George Washington departed to attend the Second Continental Congress in Philadelphia. There he was commissioned Commander-in-Chief of the Continental Army, and, except for brief visits en route to and from Yorktown in 1781, he was away for more than eight years.

MANSION AND COLONNADE FROM THE NORTH

DETAIL OF THE PALLADIAN WINDOW

In the absence of General Washington, his manager and distant kinsman, Lund Washington, continued the improvements already begun. Under his supervision the addition to the north end of the Mansion was raised and enclosed. The wing buildings and connecting colonnades were built. Forty-seven of Lund Washington's wartime letters to his employer form a valued part of the Association's manuscript collection; they record the progress of his work and his varied problems. On one occasion a British man-of-war appeared off Mount Vernon and demanded provisions. Lund met their demands, and the property was spared, although twenty slaves were carried away. On learning of this incident General Washington wrote to Lund:

I am very sorry to hear of your loss; I am a little sorry to hear of my own; but that which gives me most concern, is, that you should go on board the enemys Vessel, and furnish them with refreshments. It would have been a less painful circumstance to me, to have heard, that in consequence of your noncompliance with their request, they had burnt my House, and laid the Plantation in ruins. You ought to have considered yourself as my representative, and should have reflected on the bad example of communicating with the enemy, and making a voluntary offer of refreshments to them with a view to prevent a conflagration.

35

General Washington surrendered his commission to Congress, sitting at Annapolis, in December 1783, and turning homeward with two of his former military aides, reached Mount Vernon on Christmas Eve. Much remained to be done to the Mansion before it would be completed to the state in which the visitor now sees it, but little was accomplished in 1784. Public affairs still claimed his attention. In the autumn of 1784, General Lafayette visited Mount Vernon and is said to have been entertained in the unfinished *New Room*. Lund Washington's wartime accounts indicate that the piazza was erected in 1777, but there was a delay in finding stone flagging for the pavement. Suitable stone was imported from England and laid in 1786. The final embellishment of the house, a weather vane for the cupola, was not added until the autumn of 1787. Appropriately enough, it features the dove of peace.

Mount Vernon is an outstanding example of colonial architecture. It has much in common with other houses of the period, yet is unique in many ways. It owes its charm more to harmony of composition than to the beauty of its component parts. It has been assumed that George Washington had assistance in designing his home, and efforts have been made to identify his architect, but the assumption is not supported by the record. Architecture was not an established profession in his day, and there is no evidence in his correspondence or in his domestic records and accounts that he sought or received architectural guidance. The influence of the Governor's Palace at Williamsburg is apparent at Mount Vernon in the proportions of the wing buildings and in the bowling green, which corresponds to the palace green. Numerous similarities to other contemporary houses might be identified, but there is nothing to indicate that they were more than coincidences of style or common antecedent. General Washington had access to eighteenth-century English books on the design of country houses; the Palladian window and other details of the house, both exterior and interior, were copied or derived from one or another of these books. Here his skilled workmen may have been intermediaries since the books were written for the use of master builders. Many artisans were employed at Mount Vernon, but their work was limited in scope. It is apparent that, through the long years of development, overall planning was the province as well as an important occupation of the master. That he also supervised in some detail is indicated by the comment of a guest who

THE MANSION FROM THE EAST LAWN. CALL BELLS, USED TO SUMMON THE SERVANTS, WERE LOCATED AT THE SOUTH END OF THE HOUSE NEAR THE KITCHEN.

37

observed, "It's astonishing with what niceness he directs everything in the building way, condescending even to measure the things himself, that all may be perfectly uniform."

The most striking architectural feature of the Mansion is the high-columned piazza, extending the full length of the house, a splendid adaptation of design to setting and climate. It seems to have been a complete innovation and would, in itself, entitle George Washington to distinction among architects.

The exterior finish of the Mansion and of the courtyard dependencies is another unusual feature. The siding was beveled to give an appearance of stone; sand was then applied to the freshly painted surface. This treatment, called *rusticated Boards* by Washington, pre-dates the Revolutionary War and was used elsewhere in Virginia, but no precedent has been found for such extensive use.

The interior of the Mansion reflects architectural decoration popular from 1757 when Washington first enlarged his father's house to his last addition completed in 1787. Paint colors changed with the fashion and those now seen in the house reproduce the colors favored by Washington at the end of his life. A scientific analysis of all interior painted surfaces established a complete chromochronology from the second half of the eighteenth century to modern times. Physical evidence revealed in this study is corroborated by Washington's surviving orders for dry pigments. Wherever possible, eighteenth-century formulas and techniques of application were used in the restoration to achieve the proper period effect. Round brushes, like the kind used in Washington's time, were imported from France for the restoration, and pigments were hand ground and mixed on the estate. Where the evidence called for wallpaper, original fragments were examined microscopically and the fibers matched to English wallpapers with similar fiber construction. The paper was then applied in rectangles of approximately twenty-one by twenty-eight inches with slightly overlapping horizontal seams to simulate the appearance of eighteenth-century wallpaper. It was not until the nineteenth century that rolls of wallpaper were made in a continuous sheet.

Mansion room settings are based on a 1799 inventory prepared after George Washington's death. This fifty-page document lists the contents of each room with appraised values of every item. The appraisers were remarkably thorough, listing the subject or title of each print and painting and the title of every book, map, and pamphlet. Livestock, tools, and equipment were included for each of the five farms that comprised the Mount Vernon estate. A similar inventory, compiled in 1802 following Martha Washington's death, indicates only minor changes in furnishings during the two and one-half years of her widowhood. These basic documents are augmented by orders, invoices, correspondence, wills, early descriptions of the Mansion, and other domestic records. Because of Washington's lifelong habit of preserving his papers and the care given them by his heirs, it is safe to say that Mount Vernon is the best documented historic house for its period in the country.

THE LARGE DINING ROOM

This two-story room is most frequently designated in General Washington's writings as *the large dining room,* and occasionally as *the New Room* because it was the last addition to the house. The wing of which it is the principal part was raised and enclosed by Lund Washington, manager during the Revolutionary War. In 1776, while threatened by the British army and by the dwindling of his own military resources, General Washington found time to write from Harlem Heights to Lund of his plans for this room in the following words:

The chimney of the new room should be exactly in the middle of it—the doors and every thing else to be exactly answereable and uniform—in short I would have the whole executed in a masterly manner.

The room interior remained unfinished until the end of the war and for several years thereafter, while the master of Mount Vernon sought a craftsman who could execute the decoration of ceiling and woodwork in a manner equal to his expectations. His correspondence on the subject has been correlated with surviving physical evidence to form the basis of the present decoration. His inquiries express a preference for plain wallpaper, green or blue, with harmonizing border. The present wallpaper border was reproduced from fragments of the original, and the two shades of vertigris green are documented as the original colors. From Philadelphia in 1787, he directed that the woodwork of the room be painted a *buff inclining to white*, which might later be changed. This letter and physical evidence have determined the woodwork colors as now restored. The doors and those elsewhere on the first floor are believed to have received their "mahogany" finish in 1797 when the pine woodwork in the principal passages was grained or painted to simulate a more costly wood.

In January 1799, a young English guest noted "white chintz window curtains with deep festoons of green satin" in this room. Martha Washington identified the white material as dimity in her will. The present draping of the windows, incorporating satin and dimity of proper color and weave, follows the fashion of the period. The young guest also reported that there was "an East Indian mat" on the floor. This testimony is corroborated by an inventory, which was prepared for the General's executors early the following year.

Detail of applied plaster decoration on the Palladian window was executed in 1786 when Washington completed the interior of the large dining room.

The mantel was the gift of Samuel Vaughan, an English admirer and friend of General Washington. It arrived in 1785, as the decoration of the room was in progress. The mantel vases were also presented by Vaughan and are of English manufacture. They were made about 1770 at the Worcester factory. The decoration is the work of Jefferyes Hamett O'Neale.

Outstanding among the furnishings of this room is the pair of Hepplewhite sideboards. To the right of the Palladian window is the surviving mate of a pair made by John Aitken of Philadelphia in 1797. The matching sideboard is another Aitken piece, but has no association with Mount Vernon. Beneath the Palladian window are nine of the original twenty-four Aitken chairs made for this room.

Two eighteenth-century landscape painters are represented by the four large oils, personally selected by Washington. The rather somber views of the Great Falls and the Potomac River at Harper's Ferry, West

I have the honor to inform you that the chimney-piece is arrived, and, by the number of cases (ten) too elegant and costly by far, I fear for my own room and republican style of living.

George Washington to Samuel Vaughan, February 5, 1785

THE GREAT FALLS OF THE POTOMAC BY GEORGE BECK, 1796

Virginia, were painted by George Beck. The river scenes above the interior doors are the work of William Winstanley in 1793. The inventory, compiled after George Washington's death, lists twenty-one paintings and engravings in this room, including the representation of Louis XVI, the Trumbull engravings of the death of General Montgomery and the battle of Bunker's Hill, and the moonlight scene over the mantel.

Although identified by Washington as a dining room, this handsome space was used for a variety of functions. The absence from the inventory of a formal dining table is notable and suggests a desire on Washington's part to leave the center of the room unencumbered. A portable assemblage of trestles and boards, such as Washington used during the Revolutionary War, made it possible to accommodate large or small numbers of guests. When not in use, the pieces could easily be stored. At least two events of great moment occurred in this room. On April 14, 1789, during a brief ceremony, George Washington was informed of his election to the presidency by Charles Thomson, Secretary of the Congress, who had ridden from Philadelphia with this important news. Ten years later, by his own instruction, Washington's body lay here for three days before entombment. On that melancholy occasion, the household mourned the passing of its master.

SCENE ON THE HUDSON RIVER BY WILLIAM WINSTANLEY, 1793

DETAILS OF CURTAIN TREATMENTS, BASED ON A VISITOR'S DESCRIPTION OF 1798

ABOVE: PALLADIAN WINDOW ON THE NORTH WALL OF THE LARGE DINING ROOM, FLANKED BY SIDEBOARDS AND LOOKING GLASSES. A DOUBLE ROW OF SIDE CHAIRS STANDS BENEATH THE WINDOW. MATCHING FURNITURE PRESERVED A SYMMETRY IMPORTANT TO NEO-CLASSICAL TASTE. *LEFT:* EAST WALL OF THE LARGE DINING ROOM.

ABOVE: CHIMNEY WITH MARBLE MANTEL, GIVEN BY SAMUEL VAUGHAN, ON THE SOUTH WALL OF THE LARGE DINING ROOM. THE SCALE OF THIS TWO-STORY ROOM PROVIDED AMPLE SPACE FOR DINNER PARTIES AND OTHER SOCIAL FUNCTIONS. *RIGHT:* WEST WALL OF THE LARGE DINING ROOM.

THE PASSAGE

The passage, or central hall, as it was sometimes designated in early records, extends the full width of the house from the front door on the courtyard side to the piazza overlooking the river. During the warm season of the year, it was the most comfortable room in the house, and the journals of General and Mrs. Washington's visitors indicate that much of the informal social life of the home centered here. Under present-day conditions the passage serves as a point of vantage from which the visitor views the four adjoining rooms.

Between the doorways to the downstairs bedroom and the dining room hangs a key of the Bastille, a present from General Lafayette in 1790. In an accompanying letter the donor wrote:

Give me leave, my dear general, to present you with a picture of the Bastille, just as it looked a few days after I ordered its demolition, with the main key of the fortress of despotism. It is a tribute which I owe as a son to my adoptive father—as an aide-de-camp to my general—as a missionary of liberty to its patriarch.

I can truly say I had rather be at home at Mount Vernon with a friend or two about me, than to be attended at the seat of government by the officers of State and the representatives of every power in Europe.

George Washington to David Stuart, June 15, 1790

ABOVE: The passage where the Washingtons' guests were received. *FACING PAGE:*
DETAIL OF A PLASTER LION, ONE OF A PAIR THAT STANDS ABOVE THE EAST PASSAGE DOOR.

ABOVE: PASSAGE LOOKING WEST. WASH-
INGTON'S FONDNESS FOR LANDSCAPES IS
EXPRESSED IN THE NUMEROUS ENGRAV-
INGS HUNG IN THIS AREA.

LEFT: UPPER AND LOWER PASSAGES FROM
THE LANDING

52

The key was transmitted by Thomas Paine, who added his own endorsement of the gift in the following words:

I feel myself happy in being the person through whom the Marquis has conveyed this early trophy of the spoils of despotism, and the first ripe fruits of American principles transplanted into Europe, to his great master and patron. . . . That the principles of America opened the Bastile is not to be doubted, and therefore the key comes to the right place.

The key was presented to the Association by Colonel John A. Washington, Jr., last private owner of Mount Vernon. It is believed to have remained continuously where it is now displayed, because it was hung there by General Washington. The case is probably contemporary. The original sketch sent by Lafayette hangs beneath the key in the location selected by Washington.

Over the double doors leading to the piazza are two plaster lions, which are authenticated by Washington descendants and identified as the "two Lyons" listed in an invoice of articles received from England in 1757. The lantern and three of the prints hanging on the walls of the lower passage are identified as original objects. The other prints are duplicates of the originals that hung here in George Washington's lifetime. The fourteen chairs arranged around the walls substitute for those listed in the inventory. They might also have provided additional seating in the rooms opening off the passage.

In 1797, Washington enhanced the passage by having it painted or grained to resemble mahogany. The technique consisted of applying a base coat of a designated color over which a glaze of the desired wood color was applied in such a way that the wood grain was simulated. The pattern for this graining was found under multiple coats of paint on the door to the blue bedroom above.

DETAIL OF THE KEY
TO THE BASTILLE

THE LITTLE PARLOR

The executors' inventory of General Washington's estate lists this room as the Little Parlor. Prior to Washington's retirement from the presidency in 1797, this small chamber had been a bedroom leaving only the more formal front parlor and the passage as the principal areas for social gatherings. To compensate for the loss of a bedroom on this floor, Washington added a third one in the garret. Julian Niemcewicz, a Polish scholar, who was a guest at Mount Vernon in June 1798, wrote a very detailed and interesting journal account of a tour of the Mansion soon after his arrival, in which he states, ". . . there is another parlor, adorned with rare engravings representing sea-scenes, and here one sees the excellent harpsichord of Miss Custis."

Music played an important part in the life of the Mount Vernon household, as in the typical Virginia home of the period. The music master rode from home to home, instructing the young, and his presence often inspired lively social gatherings at which music and dancing were the principal recreations. By his own testimony Washington could *neither sing one of the songs, nor raise a single note on any instrument*, but he loved to dance, and on one occasion during the Revolutionary War, he is reported to have danced for three hours. In the second year of his marriage George Washington ordered *1 Very good Spinit* for his stepdaughter, Patsy Custis; a few years later her brother received a violin and *a fine German flute*. At a later period the granddaughter, Nelly Custis, received instruction, advancing from the spinet to the pianoforte. In 1793, President Washington imported the handsome harpsichord from London for her use. It is, no doubt, the one to which Mr. Niemcewicz refers.

The harpsichord accompanied Nelly Custis Lewis in 1802 to her new home Woodlawn, which she and her husband, Lawrence, built on the portion of the Mount Vernon estate General Washington bequeathed to them. Many years later, when it became known that the Mount Vernon Ladies' Association would acquire and preserve Washington's home, Mrs. Lewis's daughter-in-law returned the harpsichord to Mount Vernon.

The prints over the harpsichord are duplicates of marine scenes listed in this room by General Washington's appraisers. The engraved view of the engagement between John Paul Jones's *Bonhomme Richard* and the British ship *Serapis* is identified as original to the room. Here, also, is a rare trio of

FACING PAGE: Martha Washington's tea table with an Argand lamp. *BELOW*: Nelly Custis's English harpsichord is the principal piece of furniture in the little parlor.

mezzotints, small oval portraits of Washington, Franklin, and Lafayette, duplicates of those that hung here in Washington's lifetime.

The Windsor chairs displayed here replace those listed in the inventories. Though not original to Mount Vernon, these five chairs were made by Robert Gaw, brother of the Philadelphia chairmaker who made Windsors for George Washington. The cross-stitch chair cushions are reproductions of originals, which Mrs. Washington made for her own Windsor chairs. One of these original cushions may be seen in the museum. The ingrain carpeting is a reproduction of a type used in the Mansion by the Washingtons.

A TRIO OF RARE MEZZOTINTS OF WASHINGTON, FRANKLIN, AND LAFAYETTE
ARE SHOWN ON THE SOUTH WALL OF THE LITTLE PARLOR.

THE WEST PARLOR

Architecturally the front parlor is one of the most interesting rooms in the house; the door frames, the paneled walls, and the splendid mantel combine to make it one of the finest surviving examples of colonial Virginia interiors. In its present state, the room probably dates from the first enlargement of the house, just prior to George Washington's marriage. The dimensions of the *neat landskip*, ordered at that time through an English agent for use over a mantel, coincide with those of the painting impaneled over the mantel and probably determine its origin. The mantel design was inspired by a plate in Abraham Swan's *The British Architect . . .*, a popular eighteenth-century architectural pattern book. Prussian blue paint was introduced in 1787 when the Adamesque ceiling decoration was added to update the room. Prussian blue was an expensive pigment, having the peculiar property of deepening in color as pressure was applied to the brush, hence the irregular or striated effect, which showed up clearly in the microscopic examination of original paint chips.

In the pediment over the mantel is a carved and painted representation of the Washington family coat-of-arms. The coat-of-arms also appears in a decorative panel at the top of an original mirror, which hangs between the windows of the room. Washington's crest is cast into the iron fireback of the fireplace opening, one of four firebacks purchased in Philadelphia in 1787. Here the master's cipher, GW, replaces the mullets and bars in the

Above: The principal family portraits hung in the west parlor, where much of the family's social life centered. *Facing page:* Detail of the Washington coat-of-arms above the fireplace. *Right:* A portrait of Martha Washington is reflected in an original looking glass.

shield. Washington also used an adaptation of the coat-of-arms in his bookplate, which appears on page 4 of this handbook. The accompanying motto, *Exitus Acta Probat*, is freely translated, "The end proves the deed."

Before the completion of the large dining room, Washington considered this room *the best place in my House*. Here hung the more important family portraits, thirteen by the end of his life, including the first known portrait of the master of Mount Vernon by Charles Willson Peale. A copy of that portrait now hangs here, together with copies of an early portrait of Mrs. Washington and a portrait of her two children, Martha Parke and John Parke Custis. Original portraits include the five pastels by James Sharples (below) of General and Mrs. Washington, George Washington Lafayette,

son of the Marquis, and George Washington Parke Custis and Nelly Custis, the two grandchildren raised at Mount Vernon. Other originals are the Robert Edge Pine portrait of Mrs. Washington's niece, Fanny Bassett, and the Gilbert Stuart portrait of Thomas Law, husband of Eliza Parke Custis Law. The rare emblematic engraving on satin of General Washington also hung in this room during his lifetime.

The furnishings follow the inventory listing of eleven chairs, a sofa, and tea table as the only standing furniture. The urn-shaped silver lamps and silver tray were used in Washington's presidential household. The hot water urn belonged to Martha's son, John Parke Custis, and the Chinese export porcelain tea service was hers.

THE SMALL DINING ROOM

The small dining room, as it has been called to distinguish it from the dining room at the north end of the house, would indeed have been too small to accommodate the numerous guests who so frequently gathered at Mount Vernon in the years after the Revolutionary War.

An air of formality is imparted to the room by the ornate mantel and decorated ceiling, executed in the autumn of 1775 by two master crafts-men, while General Washington was in command of troops outside Boston. Lund Washington, wartime manager of Mount Vernon, wrote to his em-ployer, "The dining room will I expect be finished this week now come in. It is I think, very pretty." The extraordinary vertigris green on the walls of this room was enriched by glazing, which seems to intensify the color.

WASHINGTON'S ENGLISH LIQUOR CHEST WITH ORIGINAL BOTTLES.
AN OPEN KNIFE BOX, DECANTERS, AND SILVER GRACE THE SIDEBOARD TABLE.

SMALL DINING ROOM WITH A WINE, FRUIT,
AND NUT COURSE ON THE TABLE

Washington found green to be a color *grateful to the eye* and less likely than other colors to fade.

In accordance with the evidence of the inventory compiled by General Washington's appraisers, many pictures are displayed in this room. An engraved portrait of the Washington family by Edward Savage, and engraved portraits of two famous Philadelphians, Benjamin Franklin and David Rittenhouse, are Mount Vernon memorabilia. The others, including portraits of Generals Washington, Greene, and Lafayette, are duplicates of prints listed in the room by the executors.

The mahogany table is said to be an original Mount Vernon piece, which descended in the family of Nelly Custis Lewis, Mrs. Washington's youngest granddaughter. The table setting, which consists of nuts, raisins, port and Madeira wines, is based on a description of a dinner at Mount Vernon in February 1799, left by one of the diners, Joshua Brookes, an Englishman then traveling in the United States. Such descriptions of the Washingtons' domestic life are invaluable to an authentic re-creation of the Mount Vernon environment.

The English sideboard table approximates the original piece, which disappeared during the Civil War from Arlington House, then the home of General Robert E. Lee and his wife, the great-granddaughter of Martha Washington. Of the nine original side chairs in the room (Chippendale ladder-back type), five are identical and belong to a numbered set. The looking glass, which hangs between the windows, is another original object in the room. The handsome plated wine cooler on the sideboard table was designed to keep wines cool. Decanters were supported in baskets within the cooler and surrounded by crushed ice. The large liquor chest on the floor is believed to be one imported by Colonel George Washington just after his marriage. An entry in an invoice of that period reads as

Unless some one pops in, unexpectedly, Mrs. Washington and myself will do what I believe has not been [done] within the last twenty years by us, that is to set down to dinner by ourselves.

George Washington to Tobias Lear, July 31, 1797

follows: "A neat mahogany Square Case with 16 Gall'n Bottles in ditto with ground stoppers, Brass lifting handles and brass Casters £17.17." The purchaser felt that he had been grossly overcharged and complained to his London agent, *Surely here must be as great a mistake, or as great an Imposition as ever was offered by a Tradesman.* Such complaints were common and were inherent in the tobacco economy, which existed in Virginia prior to the Revolutionary War. The planter's cash income was derived from the sale of his tobacco crop to an English merchant. The colony exported little else, and the planter's credit with the merchant was incurred to satisfy his varied needs. Under the circumstances, delays, losses, and impositions were inevitable.

CHIMNEYPIECE WITH ENGRAVING OF THE WASHINGTON FAMILY BY EDWARD SAVAGE

THE DOWNSTAIRS BEDROOM

The downstairs bedroom was a common feature of early Virginia homes. The first reference to a bedchamber on the lower floor at Mount Vernon occurs in a letter of instruction, which the young proprietor sent on to his overseer, while journeying northward from Williamsburg with his bride in the spring of 1759. This letter is now in the Mount Vernon collection and reads, in part, as follows:

You must get two of the Bedsteads put up, one in the Hall Room, and the other in the little dining Room that use to be, and have Beds made on them against we come.

The master's bedroom may have been on the first floor until the addition to the south end of the house was completed in 1775; the surviving domestic records offer no further information on the subject.

Even after the house was enlarged, there would have been a continuing need for a sleeping chamber on the first floor. The post–Revolutionary War

family numbered eight persons: General and Mrs. Washington; the two Custis grandchildren; the General's nephew, George Augustine Washington, and his wife; and the two secretaries, Colonel Humphreys and Tobias Lear. This family-in-residence would have fully occupied the rooms on the second floor. The numerous overnight guests so frequently noted in General Washington's diary must have taxed the facilities of the house.

Room designations in the later years of General and Mrs. Washington's occupancy are more specifically recorded in several references. They reveal that there were, at one time, two bedrooms on the first floor, but that one was refurnished as a parlor in 1797, when the family returned from Philadelphia, bringing many pieces of furniture with them. This room continued to serve as a bedroom until the end of General Washington's life. The large oil painting depicts the 1759 battle of Minden in which Lafayette's father was killed. It was a gift to Washington in 1787 from Samuel Vaughan and originally hung in the large dining room before being moved here by Washington to make room for the moonlight painting that now hangs over the Vaughan mantel. The upholstered chair is an original piece and was known in the family as Martha Washington's sewing chair.

THE UPPER CHAMBERS

There are five bedchambers on the second floor of the Mansion, in addition to the master's sleeping quarters over the study. The first room at the head of the central stairway was called the blue bedroom, a name derived apparently from the color of its woodwork. A section of the original graining may be seen on the door of this room. Adjoining was the Lafayette room, so called after its most distinguished occupant, who slept here in 1784 on the occasion of his last visit with General Washington. The small room to the right of the garret stairway is the only one on the floor without a fireplace. Originally this space and the adjoining stairway had formed a storage room, which Washington partitioned when he added the garret in 1758.

On the south side of the hall is the yellow room, where an English chest of drawers, original to the room, may be seen. It was purchased by Washington in 1757 and is equipped with a writing slide and compartmented top drawer, which served as a dressing table. The Nelly Custis

For in truth it may be compared to a well resorted tavern, as scarcely any strangers who are going from north to south, or from south to north, do not spend a day or two at it.

George Washington to Mary Washington, February 15, 1787

East Front of Mansion, 1858. *By the mid–19th century, George Washington's home had fallen into disrepair. After both the federal government and the state of Virginia declined to purchase the property from the Washington family, the estate was sold in 1858 to the Mount Vernon Ladies' Association, the organization that has restored and preserved Mount Vernon ever since.*

MOUNT VERNON
The Home of George Washington

MV147
Printed in the USA

FACING PAGE: THE BLUE BEDROOM. *ABOVE:* NORTHEAST CHAMBER WHERE LAFAYETTE STAYED IN 1784.

DETAIL OF MARTHA WASHINGTON'S
CHINESE DRESSING GLASS AND TEA SERVICE
IN THE LAFAYETTE BEDROOM

room bears the name of Mrs. Washington's youngest granddaughter, who was a member of the Mount Vernon household from childhood. On General Washington's last birthday, February 22, 1799, she married his nephew, Lawrence Lewis, who had come to Mount Vernon in 1797 at his uncle's request to assist him in a secretarial and social capacity. In this room is the crib, which was used by their first child.

The walls of some of these rooms are known to have been papered originally, but the original designs have not survived. By the 1780s plain wallpaper with applied border was in fashion and Washington adopted that decoration for Nelly Custis's room and the yellow bedroom. The second floor is an interesting study of the variety of shades of Prussian blue that could be attained by adjusting paint formulas.

The Washington servants were kept busy preparing the rooms for the numerous guests who found their way to Washington's door. Mrs. Washington kept low post beds in the garret, which were brought down and set up in the rooms to accommodate the overflow. With the travelers' trunks and boxes in place, the bedrooms would have presented a busy scene.

When the Washingtons returned to Mount Vernon from Philadelphia in 1797 they brought with them "one Tin Shower bath." No other description exists, but an inventory of the contents of the Mansion prepared for Mrs. Washington's estate seems to indicate that it was installed under the stairs leading to the third floor. It is unfortunate that such a unique convenience has not survived.

INSIDE THE TRUNK, A FACSIMILE OF A LETTER IN WHICH ELIZA PARKE CUSTIS DESCRIBED HER GRANDMOTHER'S WARTIME TRAVELS

HALL BEDROOM, SHOWING WINDSOR CHAIRS

There are fewer noteworthy objects in these chambers than in the rooms on the lower floor, but a number deserve notice. On the third floor is the trunk that accompanied Mrs. Washington on her journeys to and from the winter quarters of the American army during the Revolutionary War. Affixed to the lid of the trunk is a letter in which Mrs. Washington's eldest granddaughter describes for her grandchildren how she watched her grandmother pack in the fall, "sadly distressed at her going away," and in the spring, the letter relates, "Oh how joyfully did I look on to see her cloaths taken out, & the many gifts she always brought for her grandchildren!"

There are seven rooms on the third floor of the Mansion, three of which are furnished as bedrooms to conform with the inventory compiled after General Washington's death. These provided sleeping quarters for the visitors who could not be accommodated on the floor below. On the death

At twelve I had the honor of being lighted up to my bed room by the General himself.
Diary of Robert Hunter, Jr., 1785

SOUTH CORNER OF THE NELLY CUSTIS BEDROOM.

Left and above: The yellow bedroom and detail of the chest of drawers, showing the top drawer, which is compartmented for cosmetics and other articles

Below: The Nelly Custis bedroom, showing crib given to Nelly Custis by Martha Washington.

GARRET CHAMBER USED BY MARTHA WASHINGTON AFTER WASHINGTON'S DEATH IN 1799

of her husband, Martha Washington closed the second floor bedroom they had shared for nearly a quarter century. Such tributes to the deceased were customary in the eighteenth century, but rarely for indefinite periods. Mrs. Washington moved to the bedroom in the garret that Washington furnished in 1797 when he converted a first floor bedroom into a parlor. The addition of a Franklin fireplace provided the necessary heat source for Mrs. Washington's bedroom. She continued to manage her household, and numerous guests wrote of visiting with her at this period. Her garret room was a cheerful place, and her grandson's presence across the hall was comforting. After two and one-half years of widowhood, Martha Washington died in this room on May 22, 1802.

The remaining rooms in this area of the house are identified as lumber rooms, an eighteenth-century term for storerooms. During the fall and winter months when the visitation is relatively light, the third floor is open to the public.

ABOVE: FIREPLACE IN A GARRET BEDROOM
BELOW: OVAL WINDOW IN A SMALL CLOSET WHERE
GLASS AND CHINA WERE KEPT

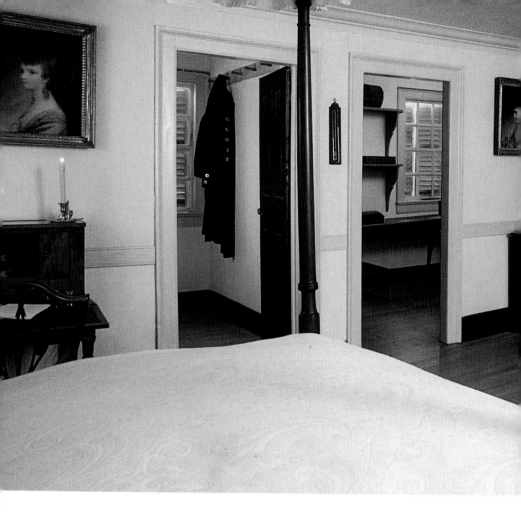

General and Mrs. Washington's
Bedchamber

This room and the adjoining closets constitute the second floor of the south addition to the Mansion. A narrow stairway from the floor below afforded the master and mistress a measure of privacy in a house constantly filled with guests.

In this room and on this bed, George Washington answered the final summons on December 14, 1799. Mrs. Washington bequeathed the bed, which she had had made in Philadelphia about 1794, to her grandson, George Washington Parke Custis. Her bequest reveals that the bed hangings were made of white dimity, a ribbed cotton fabric popular in the eighteenth century. The present dimity bed and window hangings were

MARTHA WASHINGTON'S FRENCH DESK

THE BEDSTEAD ON WHICH GEORGE WASHINGTON DIED

reproduced from an original fragment in the Mount Vernon collections. After Mrs. Washington's death, the bed was carefully preserved at Arlington House by her grandson. In 1908, through the generosity of his descendants, it was returned to its accustomed place. The unusual width of the bed and the height of the posts cause it to appear short; it is six and one-half feet long.

Mrs. Washington used this room in much the same way her husband used his study below. Management of a large and busy household took time, and she did not always have a housekeeper to assist. Here she read daily from the New Testament, and, though a reluctant correspondent, did her duty in this matter as in all others. Her French desk is probably the one listed in a memorandum of furniture purchased in 1791 from the Comte de Moustier, first French minister to this country. On top of the desk is her leather key basket, a most important accessory in her daily inspection of the rooms and buildings under her direct supervision.

The portraits are of her four grandchildren, Eliza Parke Custis, Martha Parke Custis, Eleanor (Nelly) Parke Custis, and George Washington Parke Custis. Martha and Nelly's portraits are originals by Robert Edge Pine and the others, copies of Pine's 1785 studies. The six round engravings, scenes from contemporary literature, were Mrs. Washington's selections. Mrs. Washington's knee-hole dressing table, one of the few Virginia-made pieces

When the summons comes I shall endeavor to obey it with a good grace.
George Washington to Burges Ball, September 22, 1799

in the Mansion, and the Chinese lacquered dressing glass were returned by her descendants. The easy chair is a copy of the original.

The closet on the left was used for the best linens and the one on the right for dressing and storage. The plain whitewashed walls were Mrs. Washington's preference, and the pale Prussian blue paint is a restoration of the original color. Natural pine floors, here and throughout the house, were characteristic of the eighteenth century.

A detailed account of General Washington's illness and death is contained in a letter from his secretary, Tobias Lear, which is in the Mount Vernon collection. A briefer contemporary account, from a letter published by a Boston paper a few days after the event, reads in part as follows:

The General, a little time before his death, had begun several improvements on his farm. Attending to some of these he probably caught his death. He had in contemplation a gravel walk on the banks of the Potomac; between the walk and the river there was to be a fish-pond. Some trees were to be cut down, and others preserved. On Friday, the day before he died, he spent some time by the side of the river, marking the former. There came a fall of snow, which did not deter him from his pursuit, but he continued till his neck and hair were quite covered with snow. He spent the evening with Mrs. Washington, reading the newspaper, which came by the mail of that evening; went to bed as usual about nine o'clock, waked up in the night, found himself extremely unwell, but would not allow Mrs. Washington to get up, or the servants to be waked. In the morning, finding himself very ill, Dr. Craik of Alexandria was sent for. Soon after his arrival, the two consulting physicians were called in, but all would not avail. On Saturday evening he died.

MARTHA PARKE CUSTIS
BY ROBERT EDGE PINE

WASHINGTON'S FRENCH MANTEL CLOCK

THE STUDY

The study was an important feature of the enlarged Mansion. The addition at the south end, of which it forms a part, had been enclosed under the master's direction before he departed to attend the second Continental Congress in May 1775. The interior was finished under the direction of his manager, Lund Washington, before the end of the year; the library bookpress was not installed until 1786. At that time, all the pine woodwork in the study was painted to simulate a finer wood. Known as graining, it appears elsewhere in the Mansion.

The addition to the north end of the house corresponds outwardly with that at the south end. The former was planned to provide a single large room, adequate to the demands upon the hospitality of the house. The

latter provided quarters to which the master could retire from ever-present family and company to carry on his essential activities. This room was the headquarters from which he directed the management of his estate. Here he received the reports of his overseers, made daily entries in his diary, and posted his accounts.

In this room, during the critical years following the close of the war, General Washington penned the letters that gave decisive impetus to the movement toward the establishment of a federal government. Here, at this period, was what a contemporary writer called "the focus of political intelligence for the new world." No private chamber in the land has more fruitful associations with his life at Mount Vernon. It was to this room that he came immediately upon arising, often before sunrise, and prepared himself for the day's activities. His dressing table, a French piece purchased during the presidency, stands between the windows.

ABOVE: FINE BINDINGS OF ORIGINAL VOLUMES FROM GEORGE WASHINGTON'S LIBRARY. RIGHT: WATERMARK FROM GEORGE WASHINGTON'S WRITING PAPER. BELOW: GEORGE WASHINGTON'S COPY OF ROBERT BURNS'S *POEMS* . . . NEW YORK, 1788, WITH HIS CHARACTERISTIC SIGNATURE ON THE TITLE PAGE.

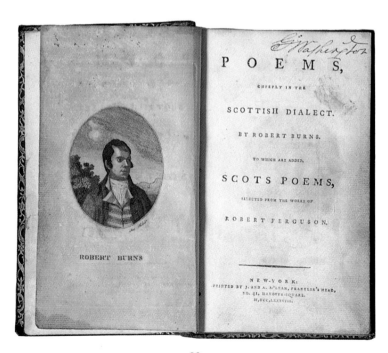

Washington's presidential desk chair and a tambour secretary made for Mount Vernon

Fan chair similar to one owned by Washington

Portrait of Lawrence Washington

Plaster profile of
George Washington
by Joseph Wright

At the close of his presidency, Washington disposed of the desk that he had used in Philadelphia, and there purchased the tambour secretary made for this room by John Aitken. The accompanying chair is also original. Desk and chair were bequeathed to Dr. James Craik, who had been closely associated with Washington since 1754 and attended him in his fatal illness. The desk remained in the possession of descendants until 1905, when it was acquired by the Association and returned to its original position. The chair was presented by the family of Dr. Craik's granddaughter to Andrew Jackson, in token of admiration, and acquired, also in 1905, from General Jackson's heirs.

The terrestrial globe, which stands near the bookpress, is an original piece, which remained at Mount Vernon and was presented to the Association by the last private owner, Colonel John A. Washington, Jr. It was made in London on General Washington's order, and reached him in New York during the first year of his presidency.

The executors' inventory lists busts of General Washington and John Paul Jones in this room. The former was the bust by Houdon, which is now displayed in the musuem. In its place here is a copy by Clark Mills. The bust of Jones, also by Houdon, was lost by fire in Alexandria many years ago; its place is filled by a copy of another bust portrait of Jones by the

same sculptor. The bas relief profile of General Washington was done by Joseph Wright in 1785 in the classical pose that became popular for national heroes after the Revolutionary War.

The whip stock on the table, the large ducking gun in the corner, and the gold-headed walking staff by the desk are authenticated as Washington memorabilia. Over the dressing table hangs a portrait of Lawrence Washington, elder half brother, which was listed in this room by General Washington's appraisers. The small walnut table is said to be the one at which the Washingtons ate their wedding breakfast at the home of the bride, where they were married on January 6, 1759. The iron chest belonged to Mrs. Washington's first husband, Daniel Parke Custis, and was used later by George Washington to secure valuable objects and papers. The barometer is said to be an original object, a reminder of General Washington's interest in all that affected his farming activities. Through the years, the state of the weather was regularly noted in his daily diary entries.

The fan chair, an eighteenth-century piece, replaced the original, which was sold out of the family in 1802. Washington bought one in 1787, shortly after its innovation by John Cram of Philadelphia for Charles Willson Peale. The fan apparatus could be adapted to any Windsor chair and was activated by operating the pedals.

The inventory of George Washington's library prepared after his death listed 884 bound volumes, numerous pamphlets, and a comprehensive collection of maps. The titles reflect Washington's wide-ranging interests and the many roles he played in his life: soldier, statesman, farmer, businessman, and gentleman. The library was particularly strong in works of

WASHINGTON'S BRASS TELESCOPE AND IRON CHEST

history, politics, law, agriculture, military strategy, literature, and geography. There is evidence of Washington's practical bent in his first order to his English agent after his marriage. Among several books requested was Batty Langley's *New Principles of Gardening*, a popular guide published in London in 1728. Langley was an early advocate of the English naturalistic style of landscape design, and Washington was profoundly influenced by Langley's theories and vocabulary in laying out his own estate. Along with his order for Langley, Washington requested a book *call'd a New System of Agriculture, or a Speedy Way to grow Rich*. Later, in Philadelphia a few days before accepting command of the Continental Army, he noted an expenditure in his pocket memorandum book, *By 5 books—Military 1.12.0*. As the war drew to an end, his account books reveal that he was seeking out works of literature and travel guides in anticipation of the leisure that would come with peace. Many of the books in the library were gifts to Washington from friends and admirers and, as his prominence grew, many American publications were dedicated to him. Washington also bought books for the edification of the many young people in his household, including Mrs. Washington's children and grandchildren and the many nephews and nieces who spent time at Mount Vernon.

Washington's library was bequeathed to his nephew and principal heir, Bushrod Washington, a Justice of the Supreme Court of the United States, together with *all the Papers in my possession, which relate to my Civel and Military Administration of the affairs of this Country [and] such of my private Papers as are worth preserving*. Judge Washington, by bequest, divided this priceless collection of books and papers between two of his nephews, George C. and John Augustine Washington. The civil and military papers were sold to the federal government prior to 1850 and are now in the manuscript division of the Library of Congress. In 1848, the Boston Atheneum acquired more than 350 of General Washington's books from a dealer who had purchased them. The remainder of the library has been widely dispersed through the years. By gift and purchase, the Association has acquired more than 75 of these scattered volumes. More than 300 of the remaining titles listed in the executors' inventory are represented in the collection by duplicates of the same imprints.

General Washington's books were customarily identified by his signature on the title page. Some also contain his bookplate, an adaptation of the family coat-of-arms. A reproduction of his bookplate appears on page 4 of this handbook. Books exhibiting the bookplate and typical signature are displayed in the musuem.

THE PANTRY

The pantry is identified in the appraisers' inventory as "the Closet under Franks direction." Frank Lee, a slave, and the son of Washington's valet, William Lee, was the butler, or steward, and occupied quarters in the basement, where there was also a white servants' dining room. The family tableware in daily use was kept here. The finer chinaware was stored in an upstairs closet. A reference in Mrs. Washington's will to "the blew and white China in common use" identifies the china that would have been "under Franks direction" in this pantry. Of this original blue-and-white Canton china, only a few scattered pieces have survived; several of these are displayed in the museum. A similar service was owned by Mrs. Samuel Powel of Philadelphia, a close friend of the Washingtons. This china has been carefully cherished and more than one hundred surviving pieces are now displayed here, the gift of a member of the Powel family.

Food was prepared in the kitchen and brought into the house by way of the adjoining colonnade. Across the ceilings of the back hall and pantry may still be seen evidence of the wiring for the house bell system, which terminated in a row of bells on the south end of the Mansion. In this way the servants could be summoned if needed in the dining room or on the piazza, where the family often took tea on pleasant days.

The closet in the back of the pantry was used by General Washington for his personal possessions. His use of inexpensive black paint in a "non-public" area was a typical economy of the great man. On the floor of the closet is an:

exact model of the Bastile, made from the very materials of this once cele-brated fortress. . . . The model . . . is admitted to be the only one of the kind in existence, except those made by order by the National Assembly for each of the Departments of France. . . .

of which there were then eighty-three. The model was a gift to President Washington from a Mr. Slade, an English admirer of Washington, and was sent to Philadelphia by Sam Bayard, whose letter of July 28, 1795, is quoted above. During Washington's lifetime, the model stood on the piazza, a plaything for the children of the household.

I wish you to have all the china looked over, the closet cleansed and the glasses all washed and everything in the closet as clean as can be.
Martha Washington to her niece, July 1, 1792

88

THE COURTYARD OUTBUILDINGS

The kitchen was the only subsidiary building on the courtyard whose designation remained constant through the years. The corresponding building across the yard was sometimes referred to as the "Servants Hall." In a letter inviting a new manager to occupy it as a family dwelling, General Washington indicates another use:

The right wing to my dwelling house as you possibly may have noticed, and heard called the Hall, (being kept altogether for the use of Strangers) has two good rooms below (with tiled floors) and as many above, all with fireplaces.

The "Strangers" were, of course, visitors, who by common custom were accorded the hospitality of Mount Vernon but who, having no credentials, were not domiciled in the Mansion. This building would also have been used by General Washington's secretaries who put his official papers in order and by the students who, during his lifetime or later, came to consult them. The first editor of his writings found them stored here.

The small building adjoining the "Hall" was listed by an assessor in 1799 as the "Gardiners House." A high turnover among free and indentured white servants, however, meant that changes in residence, based on differences in marital status and family size, were not uncommon. At an earlier period, it was designated "the Shoemaker and Taylors apartment."

The shoemaker and tailor were full-time employees, sometimes slave, sometimes white, who served the needs of the residents of the estate. In one year, the former is credited with making 217 pairs of shoes and mending 199 pairs.

The building opposite the gardener's house seems to have been used by both clerks and storekeepers and was described by a visitor in 1785 as "a well-assorted store for the use of his family and servants." From this locked depository, tools and materials were issued. An original storekeeper's account book survives in the Association's collection, and the entries afford an intimate picture of domestic economy; it was an age of handicrafts, and their products were carefully husbanded. Nails to the carpenter, oil and pigments to the painter, leather to the shoemaker, tools and seeds to the overseer, clothes and shoes for the slaves—all were carefully doled out for the immediate purpose and charged to the applicant. Also enumerated was the rum ration, given to slaves and servants as a regular part of their diet, and as a reward for particularly difficult jobs.

The posts and chains round the oval grass plot in the courtyard are restorations of original features. General Washington's diary notes that he sent a wagon *with the Posts for the Oval in my Court Yard, to be turned by a Mr. Ellis at the Turng. Mill on Pohick.* His cash account records the number of posts and ornamental drops turned and the cost of the work. On the post in the center of the grass plot is the original sundial.

MANSION AND COURTYARD OUTBUILDINGS

THE KITCHEN

By the terms of General Washington's will, the *household & Kitchen furniture of every sort & kind, with the liquors and groceries* were bequeathed to Mrs. Washington, *to be used and disposed of as she may think proper*. The large iron mortar in the scullery is identified as an original piece, which remained at Mount Vernon after Mrs. Washington's death. It was presented to the Association by Colonel John A. Washington, Jr., last private owner of the estate. The crane is thought to be an original installation; four of six pewter plates with hot-water compartments, a trivet, an iron-stand, and a bell metal skillet are also authenticated as original. Other utensils of the period, including a number from the home of one of Mrs. Washington's granddaughters, complete the collection. The Mount Vernon

kitchen utensils and other original objects of homelier character were less carefully preserved than were the finer furnishings of the Mansion; several that survive are exhibited in the museum. George Washington wrote to a friend:

My manner of living is plain, and I do not mean to be put out of it. A glass of wine and a bit of mutton are always ready, and such as will be content to partake of them are always welcome. Those who expect more will be disappointed.

Although the surviving domestic records reveal little concerning the variety, preparation, and quantities of food served at Mount Vernon, there is ample evidence that the fare was not as simple as might be inferred from the preceding quotation. After the Revolutionary War, the normal household staff included two cooks and two waiters, under the direction of a steward or housekeeper. This staff was constantly prepared to serve a large

INTERIOR OF THE LARDER

MARBLE MORTAR AND BELL METAL SKILLET

LEFT: MARTHA WASHINGTON'S
PRESERVING POT

company, and it was a rare occasion when there were no guests; several months after his retirement from the presidency, General Washington noted in a letter from Mount Vernon that he and Mrs. Washington were sitting down to dinner alone for the first time in twenty years. In another letter he wistfully told of meals at which:

I rarely miss seeing strange faces, come as they say out of respect for me. Pray, would not the word curiosity answer as well? And how different this from having a few social friends at a cheerful board! . . .

Breakfast was at seven. According to one visitor it was served "in the usual Virginia style" and consisted of tea, coffee, and meat, cold and boiled. Despite this plenty, many sources record the General's usual breakfast as "three small mush cakes . . . swimming in butter and honey" and "three cups of tea without cream." Dinner was at three. Many dinner guests have left accounts of their entertainment; one wrote:

The dinner was very good, a small roasted pigg, boiled leg of lamb, roasted fowls, beef, peas, lettuce, cucumbers, artichokes, etc., puddings, tarts, etc. etc. We were desired to call for what drinks we chose.

The choice of drinks would have included several wines, beer, and cider. General Washington's preference was for a fine Madeira wine. After dinner the host customarily remained at table for an hour or longer, conversing informally with his guests; absent friends and favored causes were toasted, in the manner of the time. Tea was served at six, and supper sometimes followed at nine o'clock—one visitor reported "an elegant supper," another that supper, a light meal, was not offered.

The hospitality of Mount Vernon was not restricted to those fortunate enough to sit at the master's table; General Washington's purse and granaries were always open to his less fortunate neighbors. Despite his long absences from home and the weight of his responsibilities, they were not forgotten. In 1775, he wrote from Cambridge to his manager, Lund Washington:

Let the Hospitality of the House, with respect to the poor, be kept up; Let no one go hungry away. If any of these kind of People should be in want of Corn, supply their necessities, provided it does not encourage them in idleness; and I have no objection to your giving my Money in Charity, to the Amount of forty or fifty Pounds a Year, when you think it well bestowed. What I mean, by having no objection, is, that it is my desire that it should be done. You are to consider that neither myself or Wife are now in the way to do these good Offices.

Opposite the kitchen fireplace are two rooms. The scullery, on the right, provided additional space for food preparation and dishwashing. The pine and spruce serving table with serpentine front is an original piece and was probably among the "kitchen furniture" purchased by Thomas Peter at the public auction that followed Martha Washington's death in 1802. Peter was the husband of Mrs. Washington's granddaughter, Martha Custis Peter,

and the table remained with their descendants until purchased by the Association. The stairway leads to two rooms used for storing kitchen utensils and as an apartment for the housekeeper. At the time of George Washington's death, the housekeeper was a white servant named Mrs. Forbes, who came to Mount Vernon after working in the same capacity for the governor of Virginia.

The second room, or larder, was naturally cooler than the rest of the kitchen by virtue of its placement partially underground. With the door closed to keep out the heat from the fireplace, perishables would "keep" here for several days. Long-term storage was provided by a nearby spring house. Over the years George Washington tried with varying degrees of success to keep ice gathered on the river for use in the hot Virginia summers. There is a reconstructed icehouse on the north lane.

ABOVE LEFT: INTERIOR OF THE STOREHOUSE WITH WASHINGTON'S PACKING CASE AND A TERRA COTTA SOAP JAR IN THE FOREGROUND. *ABOVE RIGHT:* EXTERIOR OF THE COURTYARD STOREHOUSE.

MARTHA WASHINGTON'S FAN

THE MUSEUM

The museum is a modern structure in outward harmony with the original buildings. It was erected in 1928 to house the Association's growing collection of Washington memorabilia and to provide space in which representative objects could be effectively displayed.

Here is the bust of General Washington, which was modeled at Mount Vernon by the French sculptor, Jean Antoine Houdon, who had been engaged in Paris by Thomas Jefferson, at the request of the Commonwealth of Virginia, to do a full-length statue of her first citizen for the capitol in Richmond. Houdon arrived at Mount Vernon with three assistants in October 1785. This bust, of clay, was his first model; from it he took plaster impressions for use in completing the statue on his return to Paris. The

ACCESSION POLICY

THROUGH THE YEARS SINCE 1860 THE MOUNT VERNON LADIES' ASSOCIATION HAS PURSUED A POLICY OF COLLECTING BASED UPON THE RECOVERY OF THE ORIGINAL HOUSEHOLD FURNISHINGS OF MOUNT VERNON AND THE PERSONAL POSSESSIONS OF GENERAL AND MRS. WASHINGTON. BY GIFT, LOAN, AND PURCHASE, AUTHENTIC ITEMS ARE BEING ASSEMBLED WHILE INFORMATION ON OUTSTANDING PIECES IS GATHERED AND EVALUATED. A SPECIAL FUND FOR GIFTS AND BEQUESTS HAS BEEN ESTABLISHED FOR THIS PURPOSE.

GEORGE WASHINGTON'S DRESSING CASE

ONE OF A PAIR OF PISTOLS MADE BY WOOLEY

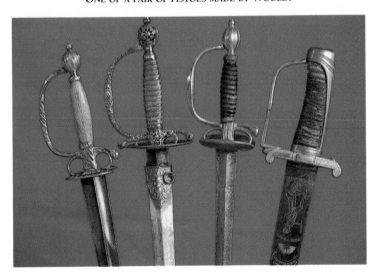

WASHINGTON'S SWORDS

TEAPOT FROM WASHINGTON'S CINCINNATI SERVICE AND A COVERED CUP WITH
SAUCER FROM MARTHA WASHINGTON'S "STATES" TEA SERVICE

CHINESE EXPORT MEAT DISH, ONE OF MANY IN THE POPULAR BLUE AND WHITE
PATTERNS USED AT MOUNT VERNON THROUGHOUT THE YEARS

MILK JUG, COFFEE CUP, AND SAUCER FROM THE NIDERVILLER SERVICE, GIVEN TO WASHINGTON BY THE COMTE DE CUSTINE IN 1782

DETAIL OF A SAUCER FROM THE "STATES" SERVICE, IN WHICH THE NAMES OF FIFTEEN STATES FORM A LINKED BORDER WITH MRS. WASHINGTON'S INITIALS IN THE SUNBURST

clay bust remained at Mount Vernon and was presented to the Association by the last private owner of the estate, Colonel John A. Washington, Jr. It portrays George Washington in the prime of his life, and was accepted by members of his household as the best among many likenesses. It has been accorded the same distinction by later critics, and is the Association's most valued possession. The bust was carefully restored in 1908.

General Washington bequeathed swords to five nephews with the injunction that they were:

not to unsheath them for the purpose of shedding blood, except it be for self defence, or in defence of their Country and its rights; and in the latter case, to keep them unsheathed, and prefer falling with them in their hands, to the relinquishment thereof.

The swords chosen by three of the nephews under this provision and a fourth, which also belonged to General Washington, are exhibited in a case next to the bust. Two of his military sashes are displayed; one of them is reported to have been presented to him by General Braddock as Braddock lay mortally wounded. The scarlet-and-off-white bindings on the pistol holsters, (page 99) here, are noteworthy as the only example in the collection of General Washington's ornamental braid.

GEORGE WASHINGTON
BY WALTER ROBERTSON, 1794

MARTHA WASHINGTON
BY JAMES PEALE, 1796

Articles of a more domestic character are grouped in the cases at the east end of the museum. Here are representative pieces of the five principal sets of china owned and used by General and Mrs. Washington. Of particular interest is the china decorated with the eagle insignia of the Society of the Cincinnati. It would have held special meaning for George Washington as first President-General of the Society. In adjoining cases are pieces of Washington and Custis silver, some of which have been loaned by a descendant of Mrs. Washington.

An ancient cornerstone with a design of halberds, heart and the initials "LW" is displayed in a small case on the south wall. Made of native sandstone, it was removed from the Mansion basement in 1910 to ensure its preservation. It is uncertain which member of the Washington family first installed the cornerstone, because George Washington's elder half brother Lawrence and his grandfather, Lawrence Washington, both owned the Mount Vernon tract.

The miniatures in the museum form an important part of the portrait collection at Mount Vernon. Two members of the Peale family, Charles Willson and his brother James, are represented by their miniatures of Mrs. Washington. Her two children by her first marriage, Martha Parke Custis and John Parke Custis, are also depicted in miniatures by Charles Willson Peale.

MARTHA PARKE CUSTIS
BY CHARLES WILLSON PEALE, 1772

JOHN PARKE CUSTIS
BY CHARLES WILLSON PEALE, 1772

SILVER COFFEEPOT ENGRAVED WITH WASHINGTON'S
COAT-OF-ARMS, MADE IN PHILADELPHIA IN 1783
BY JOSEPH ANTHONY

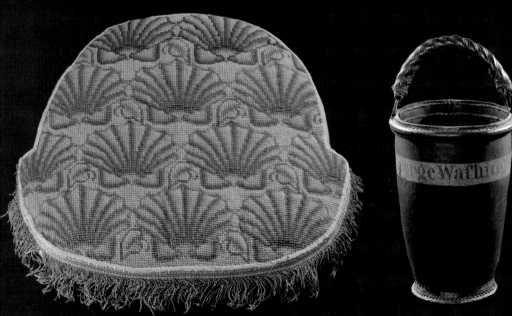

CHAIR CUSHION, ONE OF TWELVE, WORKED IN CROSS-STITCH BY
MARTHA WASHINGTON OVER A PERIOD OF THIRTY-SIX YEARS

ONE OF SIX LEATHER
FIREBUCKETS MADE
IN PHILADELPHIA FOR
MOUNT VERNON

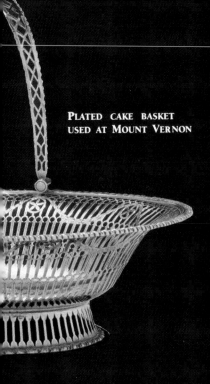

PLATED CAKE BASKET
USED AT MOUNT VERNON

WASHINGTON'S CRUET STAND
MADE BY JABEZ DANIEL IN LONDON, 1757

MARTHA WASHINGTON'S GOLD NECKLACE SURROUNDS A SMALL COLLECTION OF HER JEWELRY,
A GARNET STICKPIN, GOLD LOOPS, AND ENAMEL RING WITH PEARL

PLANTATION LIFE

"A large Virginia estate," says Washington Irving in his biography of George Washington, "was a little empire. The mansion-house was the seat of government, with its numerous dependencies, such as kitchens, smoke-house, workshops and stables." Mount Vernon is a good example of those little empires, and the orderly arrangement of its dependencies imparts a village-like character to the group of buildings around the Mansion. Yet the plan is so well managed that the service lanes do not intrude upon the area reserved for the use and enjoyment of the master, his household, and his guests. This is a tribute to General Washington's ability in the realm of architecture and landscape design. These subsidiary buildings housed many people and served a variety of essential purposes; only a carefully developed plan could have subordinated them in such proximity to the

INTERIOR OF SLAVE QUARTERS IN THE GREENHOUSE COMPLEX

main house and, at the same time, incorporated them as harmonious units of the group.

When George Washington began farming at Mount Vernon in 1758, the plantation had a work force of about twenty slaves. His marriage to Martha Dandridge Custis the following year increased the number to fifty working slaves above the age of sixteen. The earliest complete census of Mount Vernon slaves was drawn up by the General in 1786. Listed were 216 men, women, and children. One hundred five belonged to George Washington, while the remaining 111 slaves were from the estate of Martha Washington's first husband. In July of 1799, the summer before he died, Washington drafted a final census in preparation for freeing his slaves under the terms of his will. By then the population had grown to 314. Of this number, only 125 belonged to Washington, and fully 132 of the total were infirm or too young or too old to work. The 1799 census is particularly revealing in that Washington recorded ages, occupations, and

ABOVE: PLAN FOR THE GREENHOUSE WITH SLAVE QUARTERS DRAWN BY GEORGE WASHINGTON *CIRCA* 1785. *BELOW:* WASHHOUSE ON THE SOUTH LANE.

CLERK'S QUARTERS

family relationships of the individuals listed.

Mount Vernon was, as nearly as possible, a self-contained community; nothing was purchased that could be produced on the estate. Most of the wide range of skills needed on the plantation were provided by the labor of the slaves. Many of the slaves lived and worked on the outlying farms, where they were engaged in a variety of agricultural tasks. The overseers in charge of several of the farms were themselves slaves. About one-third of the working slaves were skilled craftsmen. They included blacksmiths, carpenters, gardeners, shoemakers, painters, brickmakers, and herdsmen. Others worked as house servants or coachmen. Women at the Mansion House Farm served as spinners, weavers, and seamstresses as well as cooks, dairy maids, and house servants. There were also millers and coopers, who lived and worked at the mill, about two miles from the Mansion, and boatmen, who operated Washington's fishing industry and his river ferry.

While relatively little is known about the personal lives of the Mount Vernon slaves, it is clear that the family was an important source of support and stability for the black community. The 1799 census reveals that two-thirds of the adults above the age of twenty were married and that three-quarters of the children under the age of fourteen had both a mother and a father living on the estate. Work assignments, however, sometimes meant

OVERSEER'S QUARTERS

that a mother and children might reside at one farm, while the father lived and worked at another. A few of the slaves were married to slaves belonging to other owners, and one woman was married to a free black, indicating that the Mount Vernon people could travel and visit other plantations. Food and clothing were distributed seasonally, and Washington's physician was retained on an annual basis to provide medical treatment for the slaves.

Many of the ninety slaves at the Mansion House Farm lived in the greenhouse quarters complex which, has been restored for exhibition. The slave quarters on the outlying farms have not survived, but Washington noted these people were *warmly lodged in houses chiefly of their own building.* To supplement their rations, slaves kept gardens and raised livestock for their households and families.

As a colonial Virginian, George Washington had been born into a world in which slavery was a part of the accepted order of things, but his attitude underwent a gradual evolution. Changing agricultural practices notably the move away from tobacco cultivation, had made slavery in-

creasingly unproductive and the impact of the Revolution and Washington's concern for the future of the new American nation had also influenced his thinking. After the Revolution, he had resolved never again to buy or sell a slave. *I am principled against this kind of traffic in the human species,* he wrote, *and to disperse the families I have an aversion.* Although the system continued to have a strong hold on plantation economy, by the end of his life, Washington had become convinced that emancipation was the only solution: *I wish from my soul that the Legislative of this State could see the policy of a gradual Abolition of Slavery.* The 125 slaves he owned were freed one year after his death. In his will, he also left detailed instructions for the care and support of the newly freed people and the records indicate that some lived on as pensioners at Mount Vernon for many years.

The spinning house was the most important structure on the north lane. At Mount Vernon ten or more slaves were constantly employed spinning and knitting. A number of them were physically unfit for more strenuous jobs, including "Lame Peter," Winny, who was described as "old &

SERVICE BUILDINGS ON THE SOUTH LANE

almost blind," and women recovering from childbirth. Equipment and raw materials were stored here and processed in the slaves' homes. The wool and flax fiber with which they worked were grown on the place. A surviving account book records the work of Thomas Davis, a hired weaver at Mount Vernon from 1767 to 1771. In 1768, this domestic textile industry is reported to have produced 815 yards of linen, 365 yards of woolen cloth, 144 yards of linsey (a combination of wool and linen), and 40 yards of cotton. These figures are not impressive but are unusual for the time and locality. The reels, spinning wheels, and other implements displayed in the spinning room are representative of the equipment originally used there. Some of them were collected in the Mount Vernon neighborhood over fifty years ago.

The salt-house, located just behind the "Gardiners House," provided storage space for salt and other materials used by the fishery. The extensive fishing operation Washington carried on in the Potomac was an important source of additional revenues for Mount Vernon, and there were many years in which the harvest from the river surpassed that of the crops cultivated on shore. Fishing was a seasonal activity; in the spring, when the shad and herring made their run up the river, much of the work force was engaged in netting them. Inventories indicate that scrap iron used by the blacksmith was also stored in this dependency.

The paling fences are reproduced from early views of Mount Vernon. Three small buildings, the smokehouse, washhouse, and coach house, on the south lane below the overseer's house, are open to public view. In a large household where a guest was treated "not as a stranger but as a member of the family" and the servants "took care of me, of my linen, of my clothes," the two slaves at the washhouse had a heavy workload. Examples of the laundry marks embroidered on clothes and linens for identification can be seen in the museum. The smokehouse seems scarcely adequate in size to have served the needs of the establishment. In January 1776, Lund Washington reported in a letter to his employer that he had killed 132 hogs, and remarked:

When I put it up I expected Mrs. Washington would live at home, if you did not, and was I to judge the future from the past consumption, there would have been a use for it, —for I believe Mrs. Washington's charitable disposition increases in the same proportion with her meat house.

VISTA FROM THE NORTH LANE LOOKING SOUTH

THE STABLE

The brick stable at the foot of the south lane was built in 1782, replacing a stable of frame construction on the same site, which had been destroyed by fire the previous year; it was reserved for the use of the family coach and saddle horses and those of the hundreds of people who visited the General each year. These extra animals were a financial burden and greatly increased the workload of the slaves at the stable. A young Englishman who visited Mount Vernon in 1785 noted in his journal:

After breakfast I went with Shaw to see his [General Washington's] famous racehorse, "Magnolia," a most beautiful creature. . . . I afterwards went into

If the dormant windows are not put in, one each side of the Pediment, front side of the stable, I could wish that it might be set about.
George Washington to William Pearce, July 5, 1795

his stables, where among an amazing number of horses I saw old "Nelson,"
now twenty-two years of age, that carried the General almost always during
the war. "Blueskin," another fine old horse next to him, now and then had that
honor. They have heard the roaring of many a cannon in their time. "Blue-
skin" was not the favorite, on account of his not standing fire so well as
venerable old "Nelson." The General makes no manner of use of them now; he
keeps them in a nice stable, where they feed away at their ease for their past
services.

Magnolia was an Arabian stallion that George Washington raced in Alexandria. Nelson was the valued gift of General Thomas Nelson of Yorktown.

General Washington's contemporaries testify to his outstanding ability as a horseman. The Marquis de Chastellux, who visited him at his army headquarters, says:

The weather being fair, on the 26th, I got on horseback, after breakfasting
with the General. He was so attentive as to give me the horse he rode on, the
day of my arrival, which I had greatly commended; I found him as good as he

is handsome; but above all, perfectly well broke, and well trained having a good mouth, easy in hand, and stopping short in a gallop without bearing the bit. I mention these minute particulars, because it is the General himself who breaks all his own horses; and he is a very excellent and bold horseman, leaping the highest fences, and going extremely quick, without standing upon his stirrups, bearing on the bridel, or letting his horse run wild.

Thomas Jefferson considered Washington "the best horseman of his age."

When at home the master of Mount Vernon delighted in the chase. He maintained a pack of foxhounds and hunted frequently with his neighbors; in 1768 alone, he went foxhunting on fifty separate occasions. During the hunting season the hounds accompanied him two or three times a week on his daily tour of the farms. Although they seldom failed to raise a fox, the diary often records that they *catch'd nothing*. After one of these unsuccessful encounters General Washington noted in his diary that he had *run a fox from 11 Oclock untill near 3 Oclock*.

The coach house and the coach compartment of the stable housed the family coach and a lighter vehicle, a chaise, or a two-wheeled chair. From 1768, when he ordered an English chariot *in newest taste, handsome, genteel and light*, until the end of his life, General Washington maintained a succession of fashionable carriages. None has survived. The coach in use at the time of his death was purchased by Mrs. Washington's grandson; a later owner dismantled it and distributed the parts among his friends as souvenirs of the original owner. A panel from the coach is now in the museum. One of the few surviving contemporaries of General Washington's coach is displayed in the coach compartment of the stable. It belonged to Mayor Samuel Powel of Philadelphia and his wife, who were friends of the Washingtons during the presidency and earlier. It is believed to be a substantial duplicate of Washington's coach, built by the same Philadelphia coachmaker. Washington is reported to have ridden in it while President.

The two-wheeled riding chair in the coach house is a unique survival of one of the most common conveyances in colonial Virginia. This simple vehicle is authenticated by family tradition as having belonged to George Washington's friend and patron, Thomas, Lord Fairfax. Local tax records indicate that the General paid taxes on both a light carriage and riding chair before the Revolutionary War, but he gave up the latter after the war.

Behind the stable is a shedlike extension where mules were tethered, without being confined to stalls. Among George Washington's accomplishments was the introduction of mules to the United States. Beginning with a male jackass named Royal Gift, a present from the King of Spain, an intensive breeding program was carried out under the eye of a slave named Peter Hardman. The results are evident in two inventories of Mount Vernon livestock: one taken in 1785 listed 130 working horses and no mules, the second, taken in 1799, the year of Washington's death, recorded 25 horses and 58 mules.

POWEL COACH

LORD FAIRFAX'S RIDING CHAIR

MULE SHED BEHIND THE STABLE

THE TOMB

"Within this Enclosure Rest the remains of Gen.¹ George Washington." This is the brief legend inscribed on a stone tablet over the entrance to the vault. Behind the iron gate are two marble sarcophagi, one inscribed "Washington," the other "Martha, Consort of Washington."

General Washington's will directed the building of the present vault in the following words:

The family Vault at Mount Vernon requiring repairs, and being improperly situated besides, I desire that a new one of Brick, and upon a larger Scale, may be built at the foot of what is commonly called the Vineyard Inclosure,—on the ground which is marked out.—In which my remains, with those of my deceased relatives (now in the old Vault) and such others of my family as may chuse to be entombed there, may be deposited.

The Reverend Thomas Davis, Rector of Christ Church in Alexandria, read the Episcopal burial service at the time of Washington's entombment

DETAIL OF WASHINGTON'S
MARBLE SARCOPHAGUS

TOMB OF WASHINGTON.

A CONTEMPORARY VIEW OF THE
OLD BURIAL VAULT AT MOUNT
VERNON AS IT APPEARED BEFORE
THE NEW TOMB WAS BUILT IN 1831

and delivered a brief extemporaneous eulogy. His Masonic brethren performed their graveside ritual. George Washington attended church regularly throughout his life, while at home and during his long absences. Until Pohick Church fell into disuse after the Revolutionary War, he attended there most frequently, although he purchased a pew at Christ Church, Alexandria, in 1773. Before the Revolution brought about the dissolution of the established church in Virginia, he conformed to its usages and rendered faithful service as a lay official. He continued to support its clergy during the difficult period of transition from which emerged the present Protestant Episcopal Church.

General Washington's career and writings manifest a deep and abiding faith; religion was a guiding influence in his life, both public and private. This influence is nowhere more happily displayed than in the closing sen-

And it is my express desire that my Corpse be Interred in a private manner, without—parade, or funeral Oration.

Will of George Washington, 1799

119

tence of his valedictory letter to the governors of the states, written as he prepared to relinquish command of the Continental Army:

I now make it my earnest prayer, that God would have you, and the State over which you preside, in his holy protection, that he would incline the hearts of the Citizens to cultivate a spirit of subordination and obedience to Government, to entertain a brotherly affection and love for one another, for their fellow Citizens of the United States at large, and particularly for their brethren who have served in the Field, and finally, that he would most graciously be pleased to dispose us all, to do Justice, to love mercy, and to demean ourselves with that Charity, humility and pacific temper of mind, which were the Characteristicks of the Divine Author of our blessed Religion, and without an humble imitation of whose example in these things, we can never hope to be a happy Nation.

Immediately after Washington's death Congress resolved that a marble monument should be erected to his memory within the new Capitol in the city of Washington, and that his family should be requested to permit his body to be deposited beneath it. Mrs. Washington's consent was solicited and obtained. A crypt was provided under the dome of the Capitol, but the project was never completed, and the surviving executors finally (in 1831) removed the bodies of General and Mrs. Washington and those of other members of the family from the old vault to a similar structure within the present enclosure.

In 1832, when the nation observed the centennial of the birth of George Washington, the proposal for the removal of his body to the Capitol was revived. Congress authorized application to the proprietor of Mount Vernon, John A. Washington, for the transfer, but the legislature of the Commonwealth of Virginia requested him not to consent, and he elected to abide by the intent so implicit in the will of his great-uncle.

The marble sarcophagus in which the body of General Washington now rests was presented in 1837. At that time the leaden inner casket was removed from the closed vault to the new marble and permanently entombed within it. A similar sarcophagus, more plainly sculptured, was provided for the remains of Mrs. Washington.

The marble shafts in front of the Tomb were erected to the memory of Bushrod Washington and his nephew, John Augustine Washington, who in turn were proprietors of Mount Vernon. They are buried in the inner vault. The shafts at the side of the enclosure mark the graves of Nelly Custis Lewis and one of her daughters.

Near the Washington Tomb is a burial ground identified as having been used by slaves and free blacks in the eighteenth and nineteenth centuries. A monument marking the site was erected by the Mount Vernon Ladies' Association in 1929, and a new memorial, honoring those who served in slavery at Mount Vernon, was dedicated in 1983. William Lee (*circa* 1750–1828), George Washington's personal servant during the Revolutionary War, is among those known to have been buried here.

GEORGE WASHINGTON: PIONEER FARMER

As George Washington surveyed his farms after his eight-year absence during the Revolutionary War, he reconsidered his entire method of farming. Years before, he had stopped growing tobacco and turned to grains, principally wheat. In making that change he had also built a large gristmill, allowing him to sell his produce as either grain or flour, whichever realized the greater profit. His efforts to increase productivity, however, often encountered difficulties: exhausted soil, drought, insects and disease, and reluctant slave labor.

By corresponding with leading farmers in England, Washington gained an understanding of the new theories of farming being developed there. As Washington learned about the techniques of this "New Husbandry," he resolved to pioneer them in America. At the same time, Washington purchased several pieces of land that expanded Mount

Vernon to an 8,000-acre plantation, made up of the Mansion House tract and four outlying farms. He laid out each of the four farms into seven fields to accommodate his planned experiments with the new concepts of farming. He carefully tested these ideas, and was soon directing his overseers and slaves in deep plowing to reduce erosion, fertilizing to improve the make-up of the soil, rotating crops on a seven-year cycle, sowing fallow fields in rejuvenating grass and clover, and planting crops in regularly spaced rows.

Accompanying these changes in his fields, Washington embarked on an ambitious program to improve the handling of his harvest by constructing better farm buildings. Writing to prominent English agriculturalist Arthur Young in 1786, Washington requested a plan of "the most complete and useful farm-yard," including a barn. Washington followed this plan in building a large, rectangular brick barn in 1789. With its huge size, the barn could accommodate indoor wheat threshing—normally a task conducted outdoors to provide room for the swinging flails used to beat the dried wheat plants until the grain was separated from the straw. But his departure for the presidency that year left Washington struggling to direct these changes by letter. When he visited Mount Vernon the next year, he discovered the slaves still threshing on the

THE SOLE SURVIVING PHOTOGRAPH OF GEORGE WASHINGTON'S INNOVATIVE 16-SIDED TREADING BARN. THE BARN IS BELIEVED TO HAVE BEEN DEMOLISHED SOMETIME AFTER 1870.

THE INNOVATIVE CONCEPTS THAT WASHINGTON PIONEERED IN AMERICAN AGRICULTURE ARE DEMONSTRATED AT THE FARM SITE. OXEN PULLED PLOWS, HAULED WATER AND TIMBER, AND PROVIDED MANURE TO ENRICH MOUNT VERNON'S EXHAUSTED SOILS.

bare ground, using horses in the barnyard to tread the wheat underfoot to break out the grain.

Determined to get the threshing under cover to reduce loss and keep the wheat clean and safe from weather, Washington invented a new treading barn. His design had 16 sides, making it nearly round, perfectly shaped for horses or oxen walking in a circle. Its massive timbers were strong enough to support livestock treading on the second floor, and small gaps between the floorboards permitted the wheat to fall through to the level below. Grain was collected in the lower floor and stored in central bins. Brick walls and barred windows provided security against theft. The straw left behind on the upper floor would be gathered and used in stables or for composting. The barn was built partly in an embankment, creating a gently-sloped entrance to the second floor for livestock.

George Washington's new Mount Vernon was more productive, yet required less field labor. But his attitude towards slavery was changing, and he had resolved not to sell or purchase slaves. Instead the work of the slaves began to change. Slaves became skilled craftsmen and Washington eventually identified nearly 30% of the work force as experienced in trades such as carpentry, brickmasonry and coopering. Washington expressed the hope that slavery might be abolished and implemented his own policy by freeing his slaves in his will.

Thanks to a generous grant from the W. K. Kellogg Foundation, Washington's remarkable 16-sided "treading house" is being reconstructed at Mount Vernon on a four-acre field near the Potomac River. The barn exactly follows Washington's plans and drawings from the 1790s, and the adjoining stables and corn houses that Washington designed are also being reconstructed. Every building is made of hand-shaped bricks, lumber hewed and pit-sawed to final dimension and nails hammered at an open-fire forge, just as they were in Washington's time.

In addition, the "George Washington: Pioneer Farmer" site shows Washington's innovative farming techniques. Visitors are welcome to walk among the crops, examine the fertilizers he tested, and watch horses and oxen pull cultivators and tread wheat. Washington became a leader among progressive farmers of his time, and used his position and fame to promote agricultural reform. By making Mount Vernon a showcase of these new farming techniques, he helped to introduce scientific methods to farming and bring about America's first agricultural revolution.

WASHINGTON'S 1799 CENSUS OF SLAVES, PREPARED AS HE MADE PROVISIONS IN HIS WILL TO EMANCIPATE THOSE BELONGING TO HIM. A VARIETY OF IMPORTANT SKILLS AND OCCUPATIONS ARE LISTED IN THE CENSUS.

ANN PAMELA CUNNINGHAM
BY JAMES REID LAMBDIN

THE MOUNT VERNON
LADIES' ASSOCIATION
OF THE UNION

George Washington once compared Mount Vernon to *a well resorted tavern* and indeed his home never ceased to be a mecca for visitors, drawn by curiosity or by reverence for its illustrious owner. Washington's nephew Bushrod Washington, who inherited the Mansion and four thousand acres after the death of Martha Washington, was an Associate Justice of the Supreme Court, and his duties often kept him away from Mount Vernon. He died in 1829, bequeathing the Mansion and twelve hundred acres to his nephew John Augustine Washington, who survived him by only three years. In 1850, his widow conveyed the estate to their son, John Augustine Washington, Jr., the last Washington family owner of the estate.

In the earlier years, Mount Vernon's isolation restricted the number of visitors, but by the mid-nineteenth century roads had been improved, steamboats were plying the Potomac, and the population of the country had increased fourfold. The rising tide of travel to the home of George Washington emphasized the need for its preservation. The estate was agriculturally unproductive; the Washingtons found their position untenable. John Augustine Washington, Jr., tried without success to interest both the federal government and the Commonwealth of Virginia in acquiring and preserving the historic group of buildings.

Learning of this situation, Miss Ann Pamela Cunningham of South Carolina took up the challenge. Convinced that the home of George Washington must be saved as a national shrine, she founded the Mount Vernon Ladies' Association of the Union in 1853. Through Vice Regents representing various states, the Association appealed to the American people in a campaign to raise the two hundred thousand dollars needed to acquire Mount Vernon. The people responded and, in December of 1858, Miss Cunningham and her ladies purchased the Mansion, the outbuildings, and two hundred surrounding acres from John Augustine Wasington, Jr. Restoration began immediately and the estate was opened to the public. Since that time, the Association has owned and maintained Mount Vernon under a charter granted by the Commonwealth of Virginia. The membership of the Association consists of a Regent and Vice Regents representing many of the states. The Regent, who serves as chairman, is elected from among the Vice Regents for a limited term. The Mount Vernon Ladies' Association was the first national historic preservation organization and is the oldest women's patriotic society in the United States. Its pioneering efforts in the field of preservation set an important precedent and have served as a model for many subsequent endeavors. Under the Association's trusteeship, Mount Vernon has been restored and operated without funds or assistance from the government. It is open to the public every day of the year. Washington's home has long been the nation's most visited historic house museum. More than fifty million have toured the estate in the years since the Association took charge, and, since 1950, annual visitation has rarely fallen below one million.

The year of George Washington's death, 1799, is the focal year for the Association's research programs. Although the Mansion and its principal dependencies survived, their contents had been widely scattered in the long interval between Washington's death and the acquisition of the estate by the Association. The continuing effort to identify and return original pieces to Mount Vernon is an activity second in importance only to the preservation of the property itself. Gradually an impressive number of original furnishings and personal possessions of the Washingtons, authenticated by inventories and other documents, have been reclaimed. Most of these objects are displayed within the Mansion and the museum. The Association has also assembled extensive research collections to support the work of restoration and to document the history of Mount Vernon from the seventeenth century to the present. Included are over five hundred letters of George and Martha Washington, volumes from his library, and thousands of other original manuscripts relating to their life at Mount Vernon. The Association is also engaged in archaeological research, maintains an active publications program, and co-sponsors the ongoing publication of a new, multi-volume comprehensive edition of *The Papers of George Washington*.

The preservation efforts of the Mount Vernon Ladies' Association have even extended to the surrounding countryside. The Ladies have enlarged the two-hundred acre tract they purchased from the Washingtons in 1858 by the addition of three hundred acres to guard against encroachment. In more recent years, Mount Vernon's magnificent vista of the Maryland shore across the Potomac was threatened by development. Congresswomen Frances P. Bolton, the Association's Vice Regent for Ohio from 1938 to 1977, led a campaign to preserve the pristine character of the Maryland shore, herself purchasing seven hundred fifty acres to save the land from adverse use. Through Mrs. Bolton's generosity, this tract became the nucleus of Piscataway National Park, a four-thousand acre preserve of federal and private land, created by an act of Congress in 1974.

The entrance fee and museum-shop sales provide the principal revenue for the continuing preservation of Mount Vernon. The Association has never received operating support from federal or state governments, and tax deductible contributions are welcome in order to accomplish future goals without placing the entire burden on the visiting public. Contributions assist in purchasing furnishings, manuscripts, and memorabilia associated with the Washingtons' life at Mount Vernon. The Association is also engaged in fund raising to support restoration, preservation, and capital projects as well as to establish a permanent endowment.

Today Mount Vernon is one of the best surviving examples of the plantations around which centered the highly developed social and economic life of the South in the eighteenth century. Due to Miss Cunningham's vision and the dedication of the Mount Vernon Ladies' Association, Mount Vernon remains a shrine for all who revere the name of Washington.

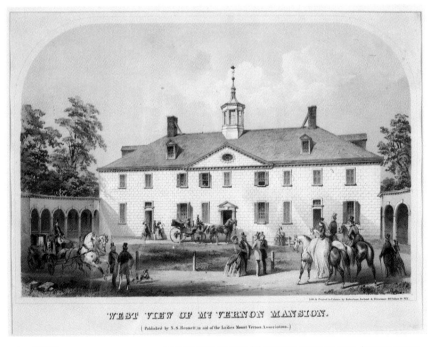

WEST VIEW OF MT VERNON MANSION.

(Published by N. S. Bennett, in aid of the Ladies Mount Vernon Association.)

AN 1858 LITHOGRAPH OF THE WEST FRONT OF THE MANSION SOLD BY THE ASSOCIATION TO RAISE FUNDS FOR THE PURCHASE OF MOUNT VERNON

A Brief Washington–Custis Genealogy

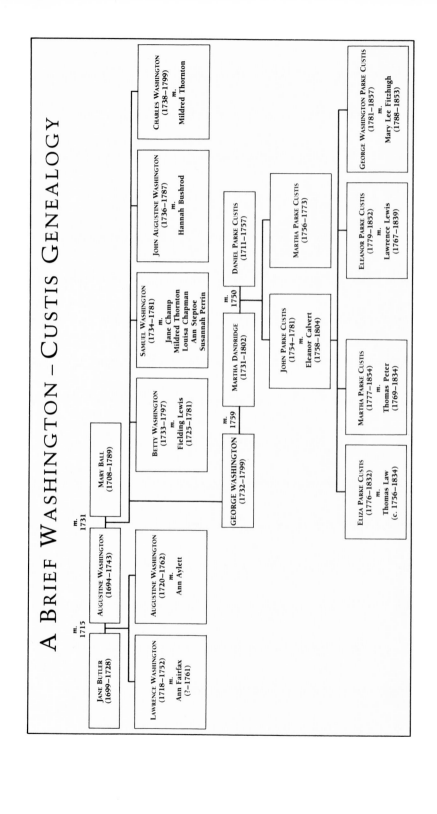

A Conjectural Evolution
of the Mansion

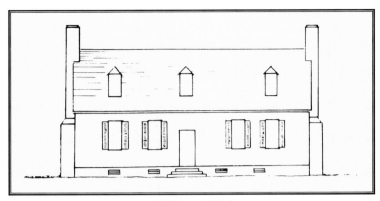

c. 1735–1758

1759–1774

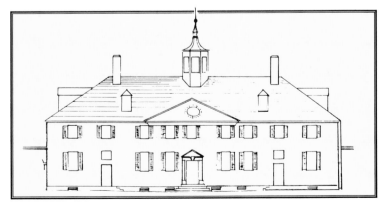

1787–1799

MEASURED DRAWINGS OF THE MANSION

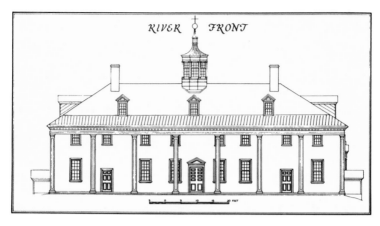

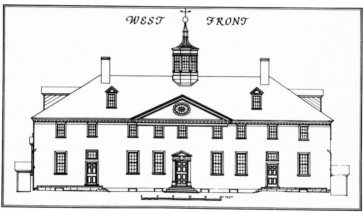

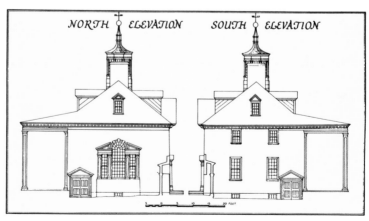

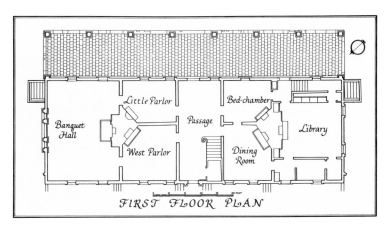

FIRST FLOOR PLAN

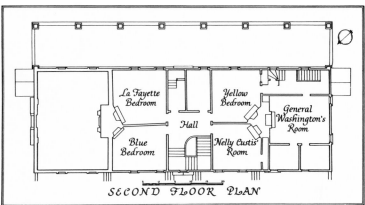

SECOND FLOOR PLAN

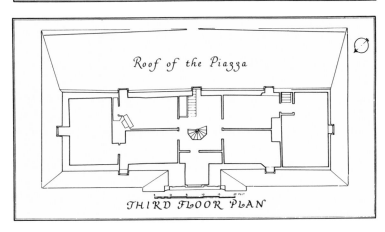

THIRD FLOOR PLAN

A PERSPECTIVE VIEW
of the
Mansion, Outbuildings, Gardens and Grounds

To East Parking Lot

1. **Entrance gate.** Tickets, maps and wheelchairs available.
2. **Bowling green** created by George Washington in 1785. Some of the larger trees survive from Washington's day.
3. **Gardener's house** was also used from time to time by the shoemaker and tailor, as well as for the sick. This building is not open to the public. A first aid center is located here.
4. **White servants' hall,** also used as an office and as a manager's residence.
5. **Mansion.** Interpreters inside explain the history of the rooms and answer questions. No photography is allowed inside (photography is allowed everywhere else).
6. **Kitchen** was set apart from the Mansion because of the heat, cooking odors and risk of fire.
7. **Storehouse and clerk's quarters** served as a center for the distribution of goods and tools.
8. **Smokehouse** where hams and meats were smoked. Martha Washington prided herself on her hams.
9. **Washhouse** where the laundry of family and guests was

washed and ironed six days a week.
10. **Laundry yard** used for drying and sunbleaching clothes and linens.
11. **Coachhouse** rebuilt on the original site in 1893.
12. **Stable** houses a rare 18th-century American coach.
13. **Paddock** held horses, sheep, mules and other livestock.
14 **Old family vault,** the original burial place of George and Martha Washington and other family members.
15. **Tomb of George and Martha Washington,** built in 183
16. **Slave burial ground and memorial** for Mount Vernon's slaves.
17. **Wharf** built in 1860. Docking location today for visitors arriving by boat.
18. **George Washington: Pioneer Farmer,** demonstration o Washington's farming innovations, including the reconstruction of his 16-sided barn.
19. **Public restrooms**, which are handicapped accessible.
20. **Lower garden** with fruits, vegetables and herbs.